Leadership

Leadership

How Real Estate Leaders Can Act Decisively to Change the Industry

Jotham Sederstrom, Caroline Feeney, and Carl Franzen

ISBN 978-1-947635-06-7 (Paperback Edition)

Printed in the United States of America
First Printing March 2018

Published by Inman Books

Contents

Foreword

Carl Franzen

"We delight in the beauty of the butterfly, but rarely admit the changes it has gone through to achieve that beauty."
— *Maya Angelou*

"That which is not good for the swarm, neither is it good for the bee."—Marcus Aurelius, *Meditations*

I don't believe that anyone is "born to lead." Or maybe I believe that we're all born with the capacity to lead, but in different ways.

My daughter Edith, our first child, is only six months old at the time I'm writing this, and she's already had a tremendous impact on me—and not just because our household revolves around her schedule.

In that short time on Earth, she's already shown me so much about humanity. Every day for an infant is a novelty, and they are constantly trying things for the first time without shame or hesitation. They don't care if they are bad at something or if they don't know "how" to do it the right way. They're also not afraid of anything. It's true, you can startle an infant, but they aren't scared of the dark (at least not at first), or looking silly, or failing.

In some ways, babies are the strongest, and certainly the most honest people on the planet. In many ways, they can teach us how to lead.

Now, I'm not suggesting that we all revert to an infantile state and that all our problems will be solved. But being a dad has re-opened my eyes to the fact that life is an adventure, an individual story that each of us is writing about ourselves. No matter where we come from and what jobs we do, we are all the leaders of our own destinies. We can't expect our lives to go anywhere, much less our careers, much less entire companies and industries, unless we are willing to try new things.

Will we get things wrong along the way? Of course. Will life get messy? Definitely, especially if you're a parent. But the bottom line is that you can't get anywhere without taking risks, being willing to fail, and being willing to learn from your failures.

I didn't have a deep knowledge of real estate when I began as editor-in-chief of Inman in the summer of 2017. But I decided to jump into the unknown, try my best, and learn from those who had come before me.

In some ways, the transition was smoother than I expected. Like journalism, real estate is in the midst of an extraordinary transformation thanks to technology. People have never had access to more data and more options for servicing their housing-related needs.

At the same time, economic, sociocultural, and environmental forces are exerting pressure on the housing market in unpredictable ways. These present new challenges for people who work in the real estate industry. But at its core, real estate remains about the same things it always has: people and the places they call their own. And as long as there are people looking for places to buy and sell, they will need guides to show them the way.

In the modern real estate industry, that guide may take the form of an app, an artificial intelligence assistant, or a fellow house-hunter or seller leaving an online review. There are many new ways in which technology is augmenting the experience of buying and selling properties.

The question for leaders in real estate at every level, from the self-starting agent to the brokerage owner to the CEOs of the biggest companies is: how to best leverage new technologies and the opportunities they present without being overtaken or undercut by them?

A similar line of inquiry can be applied to sociocultural and political movements too, like the #MeToo movement now spreading from Hollywood across various industries. In the case of this movement, it's clear that leaders failed to create a hospitable environment free of sexual harassment and misconduct, or in some cases, actively perpetuated abusive acts against people who trusted them. A major question for all leaders across industries going forward is: how to create safe spaces for all those who work with them, and regain the lost trust? Also pressing: how to make sure that leaders don't abuse the power they're given?

The physical environment is changing all around us, too. The sea level and carbon emissions are rising, and with them come changes in the very living spaces the real estate industry seeks to provide. Even if you don't accept the consensus around climate change, it's clear that natural disasters such as the series of hurricanes and wildfires that buffeted the Americas in 2017 will continue testing leaders in the public and private sectors—how to rebuild and prepare for the next storms?

Perhaps most acutely for those in the real estate industry, there is the economic challenge of affordability. Since the financial crisis, we've been on a long road to recovery. Thankfully at the time of this writing, statistics show that the home values wiped out in the recession have been regained. But the truth is that those gains have been uneven, and homeownership is a fading dream for many Americans. What can real estate professionals do to make housing more accessible?

How can real estate leaders rise to meet all these challenges? That's the essential question we sought to answer with this project. But instead of asking real estate leaders, we turned to our community of readers at Inman News and asked them in the form of a 61-question online survey, dozens of interviews, and by giving them the space to respond in our comments, articles, and over email. What you're about to read is the culmination of that project, which we called Leadership Week.

Of course, there are no easy answers to these difficult questions. But if there is one takeaway that emerged from all of our reporting and research, I think it's this: the best leaders are those who are most willing to learn—even when the lessons are tough. And that true leadership means being open to learning from people at all levels, in all walks of life. That was the genesis of this project—asking people who lead from the bottom up what the leaders on top could be doing better.

Even the youngest and most inexperienced among us—babies, for example—have something to teach us. I hope that this book, and the knowledge contained herein, can help us all to be as open

and eager to learn the world as we were when we were first came
into it.

Introduction

The real estate industry must rethink leadership from the ground up as deep rumblings of change begin to crack the surface, threatening to rupture tradition and leave an array of legacy companies in the dust. The top-down, exclusive pyramid model is no longer suited for a dynamic and evolving business.

In some ways, everyone is their own leader in an industry made up of two million independent contractor real estate agents who have the opportunity to drive their own destiny. This creates an innately flat structure at odds at times with old-school top-down brokerage cultures and organized real estate's hierarchy that instead should reflect a diverse tapestry of ideas, backgrounds and strengths through a more collaborative, responsive and team-driven model.

"We are too busy being captains of our own destiny to really notice who is leading what and why," commented Minnesota broker-owner Teresa Boardman.

In a deeper exploration of real estate leadership, Inman flipped the script by surveying 787 industry professionals over a 10-day period in February about what they'd like to see happen at the top, while inviting the industry's movers and shakers to contribute their ideas through a series of articles, Q&As and social posts and inquiries, all of which you'll find compiled here in this book.

What we learned through this aggregation of insights is that now more than ever we need new forms of leadership, a new generation of leaders and a new compact among them to bring the industry into a new age driven by transparency, authenticity and the courage to face competitors in fresh, creative ways. The appetite for change is strong—an informal Facebook Group poll asking Inman's readers "what's one thing you'd change about the industry?" incited nearly 120 comments calling for improved leadership, raising barriers to entry to an overcrowded field, and better benefit offerings from brokerages.

"There is hope for current leaders if they accept this atmosphere of high visibility and rapid change, and seek to inspire success and responsibility in an environment that will require both," wrote Seattle managing broker Sam Debord in an article exploring how transparency will transform real estate industry leadership. "Moves toward a philosophy of openness are being seen even in the industry's most long-standing organizations."

Technology that helps and hurts progress

According to Inman's research, the biggest threat to traditional real estate is an ambush on multiple fronts from consumer-direct upstarts, on-demand apps and other data-driven tech disruptors.

Moreover, the industry's attempt to leverage technology to its advantage has thus far been piecemeal and oftentimes off the mark. It's true that real estate professionals are successfully integrating new technology with traditional sales strategies and are calling on leaders to more quickly embrace cutting-edge digital platforms, apps and lead generation tools to stay competitive.

But many agents reported lackluster products and long-term contracts, not to mention a flash-in-the-pan lifecycle for some tools that fall out of favor at lightning speeds.

"Adopting poor technology and then being tied into a long term contract compounding the poor decision," a Tahoe City, California, Realtor wrote, balking at questionable tech purchases.

Diversity in hiring and leadership

The research offered cause for hope, namely the positive sentiment expressed by real estate professionals about their leaders' commitment to diversity. Fifty-five percent of respondents reported that leadership at their company was "very committed to diversity," and another 31 percent said it was "somewhat committed to diversity" in the workplace. Only 3.7 percent claimed executives weren't committed at all.

Still, 40 percent of those polled said that even the most committed leaders could do more in terms of hiring. In a female-dominated industry run by mostly men at the top, there's no doubt that more balanced gender representation is needed.

Between 2011 and 2015, the most recent year in which comprehensive industry-wide numbers are available, executive leadership positions among women remained unchanged at 26 percent nationwide, according to Real Trends, the Colorado-based real estate consulting firm.

"We actually see real estate firms doing slightly better than, say, hedge funds in getting more women through the door and working in those companies," said Amy Bensted, head of hedge fund products at Preqin, who co-authored a 2017 report on women in alternative assets. "We see higher levels of C-level representation. But the real picture is that females are still grossly underrepresented."

Furthermore, with the dawn of the #MeToo movement and raised awareness of sexual harassment in the workplace, Inman found that allegations of sexual harassment and misconduct by senior leadership do exist across the industry in brokerages large and small, but they are relatively rare, standing in contrast to otherwise mostly positive depictions of real estate leadership nationwide.

A new type of leader

The challenges may sometimes seem daunting: a wave of warp speed tech shifts, a vexing housing affordability problem, new dynamics in the workplace and social and political unrest around us.

Trulia co-founder Pete Flint recently warned the industry of the unstoppable "tsunami of disruption" that will kill the majority of traditional real estate companies within the next 10 years. Berkshire Hathaway HomeServices agent Jake Breen fears the day when "one big conglomerate"—whether it be Zillow and Amazon, or Zillow and Google—announce a consumer-direct model and "it's game over: no more real estate industry" as we know it.

These are problems that leaders can confront if they act decisively and join together. Take the issue of open data—rather than forming a united front, the industry is fragmented with a gaggle of groups and companies taking a different position.

But real estate can no longer sit idly by, squabbling on the fringe and divided in factions trying to trip each other up. It must insist on diversity in leadership positions. It must stand up to challenges like affordable housing and natural disasters and climate change, and it must join hands to embrace open data and not discourage disruptors. It should charge hard for higher agent standards and a stronger code of ethics. It should work to meet new consumer expectations of speed, convenience and certainty.

"The current generation of leaders must be willing and able to ask hard questions and make tough decisions that won't make him or her popular, but will result in saving the real estate industry as we know it," writes industry consultant Robert Hahn in his thought piece, "Leadership in real estate: Courage is what we need."

Examples of leadership excellence

Some leaders in the brokerage, technology and mortgage spaces are already forging a new path in the right direction.

Top NYC brokerage leader Elizabeth Ann Stribling-Kivlan knows all 330 real estate agents who work for her and requires each one of them to go through diversity training to create a company culture of inclusion. Formal rabble-rouser turned real estate industry ally Glenn Kelman said what keeps him up at night is concern over the needs of Redfin's homebuyer and seller customers, and whether they are being met first.

As CEO of fast-growing brokerage Compass, Robert Reffkin openly shares his failures with his company so they can learn from mistakes faster. Concierge Auctions founder Laura Brady drives her team toward a higher purpose—for every home her company sells, it funds a home for a family in need.

Commissions, Inc. founder Duane LeGate sold his company and shared much of the gains with every employee, even though he was not obligated to. He rewarded the flat org.

Three members of the Austin Association of Realtors sued the trade group to overthrow the old guard who allegedly were not acting in the best interest of its members. They demanded transparency and power to the members.

Jillayne Schlicke publicly called out a mortgage executive who opened a presentation with a homophobic joke. She understands the first step towards diversity is by wiping out bigotry and prejudice.

Keller Williams' John Davis and Gary Keller canceled their convention to make way for the attendees to do volunteer service in the Houston natural disaster zone. The power of the network was more important than the fat cats showing off their ideas and predictions.

According to our research, these leaders reflect something that the industry would like to see more of—whether it be transparency, a higher commitment to social good or a strong company culture.

'We owe it to our agents to be relevant'

Our readers do not necessarily expect their leaders to be crusaders but want advocates for the issues they believe will most impact the real estate industry—affordable housing, health care, tax reform, government regulations and agent safety. Lean into social causes, including disaster relief—but keep your political views to yourself, they warn. Most of all they want to be invited to the conversation, for leaders to break out of their ivory towers and listen.

Because preaching support of agents is an empty promise unless you build a business around their success. Espousing innovation but unfairly blocking disrupters is hypocrisy. Defending associations but failing to hold them accountable is politics at their worst.

Indeed, the real estate industry is a powerful force made up of many brilliant minds, bold voices and a tenacious, scrappy rank-and-file. Can it face its blind spots and adapt, or will it accept a fate like Blockbuster, bricks-and-mortar retail and the music industry in the years to come?

In the words of Century 21 CEO Nick Bailey: "To be competitive, we owe it to our agents to be relevant today and tomorrow."

The choice is yours, and the time is now.

The Parker Principles: A Real Estate Manifesto

In the spring of 2018 in Palm Springs, California, a diverse collection of real estate innovators, leaders and influencers gathered to hammer out a manifesto for changing the real estate industry. They were guided by the mandate of creating a better and more certain consumer real estate experience.

1. Transform our industry from a sales profession to a service business

Incentivize real estate agents to focus on quality and service over volume and sales by obsessing over the needs of the consumer to drive innovation and best practices.

2. Simplify the process of buying and selling a home

We must make the transaction smoother and simpler throughout the process. Create more transparent transaction management tools to give consumers a better and more certain experience.

3. Create a transparent chain of industry accountability to benefit the consumer

From associations/MLSs to brokers, brokers to agents, and brokers and agents to consumers, we must hold the industry to a higher standard of service, transparency and responsibility. The core of accountability is transparency across the industry.

4. Strictly enforce ethical standards to increase professionalism

We as a profession owe it to the consumer to establish—and maintain and enforce—the highest standards of ethical behavior. We must invest in mid-level real estate manager training; refocus culture and policies toward quality and service above recruiting and retention in the brokerage; and establish better peer-based enforcement mechanisms to weed out bad apples.

5. Raise the quality of real estate services to create a delightful and more certain consumer experience

We must take ownership of competency. Create better and more experiential educational systems such as apprenticeships that allow unproductive agents to learn from peers, as well as higher and more meaningful standards in licensing/accreditation. Ensure more transparent information to consumers to allow them to evaluate real estate professionals and be more selective in choosing an agent.

6. Demand real estate associations be more transparent and impactful

We should create a culture and process that ensures every association member has an equal opportunity to be fully informed of key issues and to lead the organization. Focus money and effort on creating a healthy real estate market. Simplify the association's role to a focus on creating opportunities for agents to sell more real estate. Encourage agents to take a more active role in their communities to make a difference in housing costs and community quality of life.

7. Free up property data feeds and remove barriers for innovators

We should create a world where property data can be used, reused and broadly distributed. Remove artificial and overly protective barriers to property data access and utilization via a universal licensing agreement. Remove artificial barriers to new ideas, inventions and business models that improve the real estate experience.

8. Insist on diversity in real estate leadership

We must create an industry proudly known for inclusion and diversity. In the boardrooms, in the executive suite, on stages and in strategy gatherings, the industry at the top must reflect the overall diversity of business. A new generation of leaders are ready to take over and they should be celebrated and empowered to do so.

9. Fight for more "available" housing

We must bring key stakeholders to the table including builders, policymakers, associations and real estate professionals to build more entry-level units and mixed-housing projects to create more balanced, affordable markets and bring relief to the many Americans on the verge of homelessness.

10. Make our communities better places to live and work

We should use our influence as real estate leaders to give back and advocate for and support education (even if it means higher taxes), marginalized communities and policy that will promote affordable housing and access to homeownership in the long term.

11. Selflessly give back to the world through service

We must recognize the importance of building service into our companies, organizations and our brand to authentically give back to the world beyond our own community.

12. Stand up to climate change and prepare for natural disasters

The industry must stand up for sustainability and commit to disaster preparedness. The industry should equip their clients with the knowledge to be responsible in using natural resources wisely and supporting a sustainable community. We must make sure that our teams and their clients have taken the steps to be resilient in the face of extreme weather events and emergencies. We must be transparent with clients about the threats of nature, fully disclosing changes in the environment.

1.

Publisher's Note: A Blueprint for Real Estate Change

Brad Inman

In 1992, I joined a progressive group of architects and designers for a gathering at the breathtaking Ahwahnee Lodge in Yosemite, California. We rallied around the idea of dense urban neighborhoods that were walkable, diverse and affordable—a "new urbanism". Those at the Lodge that weekend more or less agreed with one another about that lofty mission.

And the differences did not get in the way of us forging the Ahwahnee Principles, 15 bold notions about how to create better communities. Some of us spoke up, some argued and others listened, but in the end there was a loosely agreed to, unofficial, set of principles (read the full list below).

For two decades, the ideas were passed along to cities, planners and activists around the country and they have played a part in a new future for cities. Official groups of all kinds embraced these ideas. How they were shaped was part of their idyllic appeal.

Ideas are powerful. More powerful is the right people agreeing to specific ideas and pledging to make them work.

The Ahwahnee Principles are a blueprint for what I believe we can accomplish in the real estate industry—a different set of problems with a different set of leaders and activists.

But imagine a strong, influential and scrappy group of people getting together, listening to the input of real estate professionals, and pledging to make the real estate industry a more open, inclusive and courageous force—one that will usher in changes that make the consumer real estate experience better.

Such a group is being brought together this month to forge a new compact for changing the real estate industry. Let's call it A Declaration of Freedom from the Old Ways.

- Imagine an agreement on open data.

- Imagine a transparent NAR

- Imagine a courageous industry wide effort on affordable housing

- Imagine an industry compact on climate change

- Imagine a National MLS database

- Imagine higher standards for professionalism and a stricter code of ethics for NAR

- Imagine diversity in the executive suite of real estate companies and associations

- Imagine unconstrained competition in which innovation is encouraged not thwarted

So much to do, but all within the industry's reach. If such a compact is successfully created, this book will be edited to reflect the group's thinking. Then the real estate industry can march ahead making changes that we all know are important and helpful for the future.

The Ahwahnee Principles

1. All planning should be in the form of complete and integrated communities containing housing, shops, work places, schools, parks and civic facilities essential to the daily life of the residents.

2. Community size should be designed so that housing, jobs, daily needs and other activities are within easy walking distance of each other.

3. As many activities as possible should be located

within easy walking distance of transit stops.

4. A community should contain a diversity of housing types to enable citizens from a wide range of economic levels and age groups to live within its boundaries.

5. Businesses within the community should provide a range of job types for the community's residents.

6. The location and character of the community should be consistent with a larger transit network.

7. The community should have a center focus that combines commercial, civic, cultural and recreational uses.

8. The community should contain an ample supply of specialized open space in the form of squares, greens and parks whose frequent use is encouraged through placement and design.

9. Public spaces should be designed to encourage the attention and presence of people at all hours of the day and night.

10. Each community or cluster of communities should have a well defined edge, such as agricultural greenbelts or wildlife corridors, permanently protected from development.

11. Streets, pedestrian paths and bike paths should contribute to a system of fully connected and interesting routes to all destinations. Their design should encourage pedestrian and bicycle use by being small and spatially defined by buildings, trees and lighting; and by discouraging high-speed traffic.

12. Wherever possible, the natural terrain, drainage, and vegetation of the community should be preserved with superior examples contained within parks or greenbelts.

13. The community design should help conserve resources and minimize waste.

14. Communities should provide for the efficient use of water through the use of natural drainage, drought tolerant landscaping and recycling.

15. The street orientation, the placement of buildings and the use of shading should contribute to the energy efficiency of the community.

2.

The essential guide for real estate leadership on tech disruption

Jotham Sederstrom

The biggest threat to traditional real estate is neither a dearth of inventory nor a volatile stock market, but an ambush on multiple fronts from consumer-direct upstarts, on-demand apps and other data-driven tech disruptors, according to Inman's inaugural survey asking the industry rank-and-file how their leaders could be doing better.

Nearly 30 percent of 787 real estate respondents polled for Inman's survey on real estate leadership in February said "technological disruption" remains the single biggest threat to the real estate industry, edging out other perils like shifting demographics, market fluctuations and global politics.

And while nearly 85 percent of real estate professionals have faith that leadership within their companies are up to the challenge, more than 15 percent said they're less hopeful.

"Believe me, I don't want to spit in the face of what I do for a living, but I believe [the real estate industry] has changed a lot in the last five years and it's going to change drastically in the next five," said Jake Breen, a Berkshire Hathaway HomeServices agent in Utah. "My worry is that it only takes one big conglomerate—Zillow teaming up with Amazon, or Google—to announce they're starting a consumer-direct model, and it's game over: no more real estate industry."

The biggest threat to real estate today is:

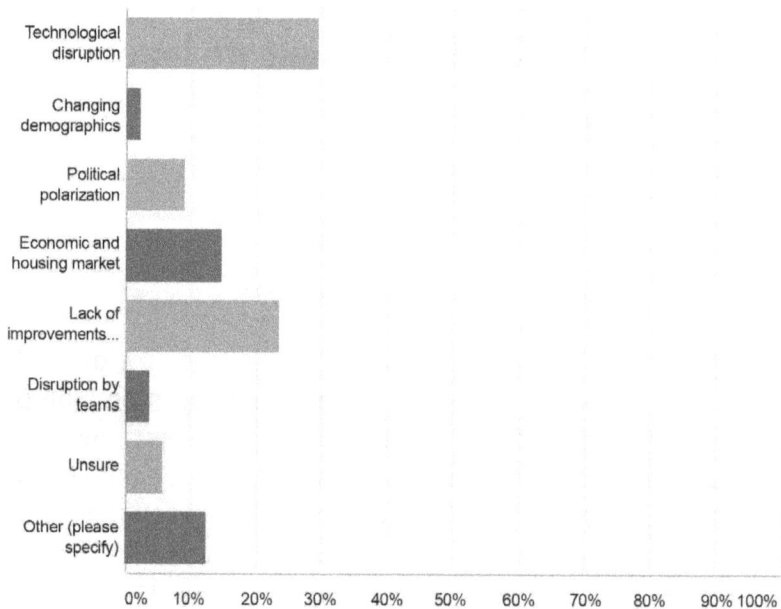

What leaders need to know to stay ahead

Anxiety over tech disruption comes as venture capitalists are increasingly turning their attention to the real estate industry. In 2017, investors shoveled more than $5 billion into real estate tech upstarts like Opendoor, Compass and other would-be barbarians at the gate, up from $33 million less than a decade earlier, according to Pitchbook, the private equity research firm.

The renewed interest from investors also coincides with a new generation of millennial homebuyers entering the market, many of them tech savvy and unafraid to seek out information online.

More than 70 percent of real estate professionals polled believe their leaders are prepared for the new generation, while 29 percent worried their strategies need fine-tuning.

"[Leadership needs to] adopt a business model that better serves the needs of our demographic as well as millennials and gen-

Xers," one Florida agent wrote, adding she doubts executives at her company understand the latest industry trends. "One that incorporates more online interaction as well as a higher standard of service to improve the customer experience."

How well do you think your leadership understands
new trends shaping your business?

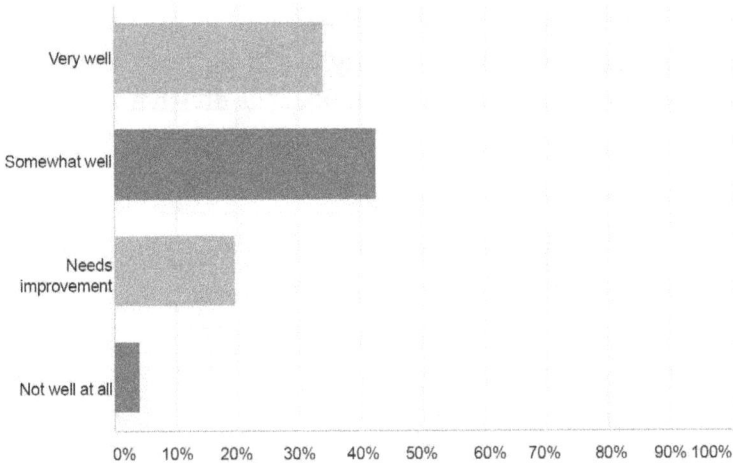

Breen, a broker advisor for REthink, the millennial think tank launched by Berkshire Hathaway HomeServices in 2013, warned that young homebuyers are just now beginning to feel comfortable eschewing brokers for a consumer-direct rival like Opendoor and data-driven sites like Zillow and Trulia, both of which stoked fears when they launched more than a decade ago.

"My worry is consumer mindset—what they think about us as an industry—has finally caught up," Breen told Inman News. "I have good friends, people who still won't transact without my advice—but just my advice, not my services. Data is so easy for them now that we're starting to see the millennials and Gen Xers becoming the big buying group. They're finally comfortable enough to transact online. The tools are getting good enough for them to trust whoever connects with them on the phone—whether it's a Zillow representative or a discount broker."

Should real estate leaders spend energy resisting Zillow?

With Zillow in mind, real estate professionals overwhelmingly agreed that industry leaders, both within their company and at the helm of trade associations, should actively resist the Seattle-based online database, according to the Inman News survey. Nearly 60 percent believe leaders should take control of listing data from Zillow and other consumer-facing websites.

Real estate professionals also weighed in on other potentially disruptive shifts in the industry, including a divisive push for a national multiple listing service, to which nearly 60 percent of respondents were opposed. About 33 percent, meanwhile, were in favor of a national MLS.

"I can see the pluses and negatives for both," said Sean Thomas, an agent with eXp Realty in California. "Canada has one national MLS and they love it, and the MLS looks out for the best interests of their agents and their population. If we were able to emulate that, and actually really follow that as a model, that would be phenomenal and I would agree to a national MLS."

Thomas is among an emergent group of Realtors banking on the disruptive potential of technology in the real estate sector. In 2015, he launched "Show Me Now," a GPS-powered on-demand real estate app he describes as "the Uber of real estate" that allows potential homebuyers to bypass slow-to-respond listing agents who aren't immediately available to show nearby homes on the market.

By his estimate, the app currently boasts about a hundred cooperating agents across North America and elsewhere who have signed on to show properties to potential buyers when listing agents aren't readily available, he told Inman News.

How well do you believe your leader understands the needs
of new generations of clients and business partners, such as
millennials and Gen Z?

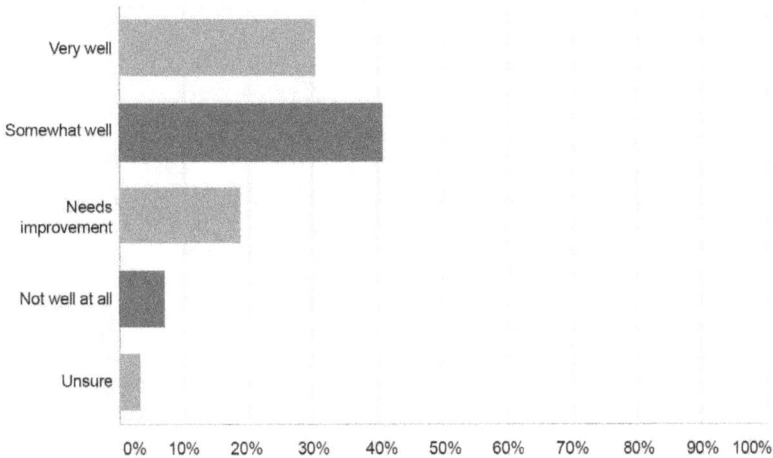

"Broadly speaking, on-demand technology is very disruptive right
now, just because it's putting a lot of agents in check," said
Thomas. "Real estate agents love their ability to make their own
schedule, and clients more and more—it used to be just millennials—want things right now. And with everything that's out
there—Uber, [California delivery service] Foodjets, you name
it—it's turning more and more into that service-based industry. So
why not real estate?"

3.

The essential guide for real estate leadership on sexual harassment and gender

Jotham Sederstrom

The allegations of sexual harassment and misconduct by senior leadership, lobbed against brokerages large and small from Washington state to the District of Columbia, stand in stark contrast to otherwise mostly positive depictions of real estate leadership nationwide. But it's there—laid out bluntly in Inman's first ever Real Estate Leadership Survey of more than 780 real estate professionals.

Stories of inappropriate behavior by leaders

"Constant partying and drinking," one marketing professional in Orlando, Florida, claimed, referring to senior executives at her company. "Affairs with younger staff, who they fire when they become a problem for them. Refusing to accept responsibility for anything. Delusions of grandeur. Inappropriate use of office and corporate equipment. Wasting vast amounts of money on entertaining themselves."

"[He] comments on my leather pants," yet another Long Island, New York-based Realtor alleged, describing a senior executive at her residential brokerage firm. "[He] asks me who I would fuck in the office…. and so on. [He] interrogates people to get it out in a friendly way."

"There is a culture of sexual harassment with our management," a Seattle-based agent added.

The comments, tucked inside Inman's wide-ranging, 61-question leadership survey and often submitted anonymously, were posted by a minority of real estate professionals who believe that sexual harassment and bad behavior run rampant in an industry led largely by older men.

Set against the wider, women-led #MeToo movement against sexual harassment and misconduct, brought on in the aftermath of dozens of allegations of sexual assault leveled against movie producer Harvey Weinstein, the claims against top-level real estate executives are unsubstantiated for now, but aren't so easy to ignore nor explain.

But most say leaders act appropriately

Asked if leaders within their companies engage in inappropriate behavior, only 7.9 percent said "yes," with a whopping 88.2 percent voiced a resounding "no." Another 10 percent said they were "unsure" if senior executives engaged in bad behavior, according to results of the survey.

Does the leadership of your company engage in inappropriate behavior?

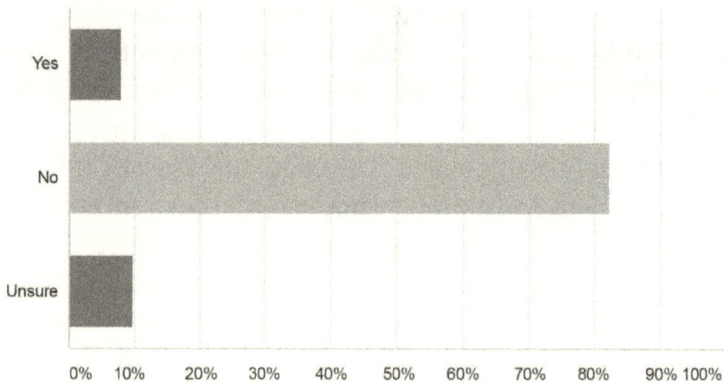

	Percentage
Yes	
No	
Unsure	

0% 10% 20% 30% 40% 50% 60% 70% 80% 90% 100%

Meanwhile, 76.8 percent of real estate professionals characterized their company's position on sexual harassment as "fine as it is."

Another 4.7 percent said company policy was "not strict enough" and, somewhat curiously, a little under 1 percent said their policy was "too strict."

How would you characterize your company's position on sexual harassment or other forms of sexual misconduct in the workplace?

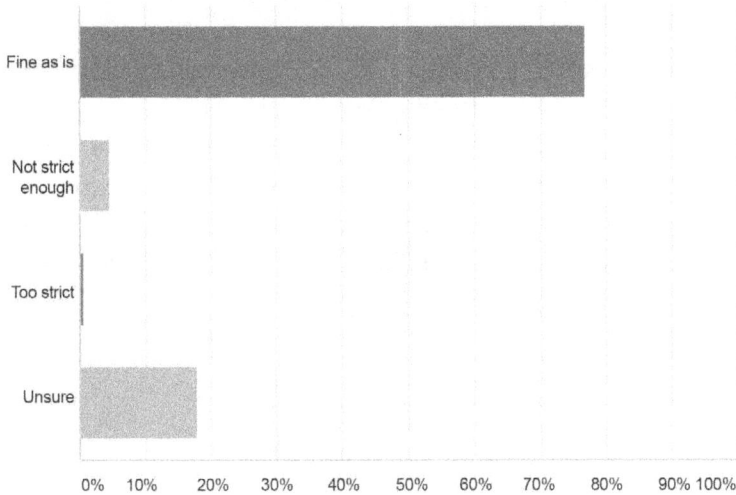

"This is an old-school industry," wrote one marketing associate for a lender in Washington. "It's a boys club. Us women have to play the game, be like one of the boys, to succeed."

Women remain scarce in leadership

The conversation comes as a renewed effort to elevate women in leadership positions is gaining momentum from initiatives like the California Association of Realtors' Women Up campaign, which aims to lift women into the highest echelons of the real estate industry.

In states like California, where only 14 of the top 100 brokerages are owned by women, the lack of diversity is conspicuous. But across national franchises, too, the numbers are problematic.

Between 2011 and 2015, the most recent year in which comprehensive industrywide numbers are available, executive leadership positions among women remained unchanged at 26 percent nationwide, according to Real Trends, the Colorado-based real estate consulting firm.

Globally, the number of senior level positions held by women stands at 10 percent, according to a report release in October by Preqin, an alternative assets data provider headquartered in Manhattan and London. The report, "Women in Alternative Assets," also found that, globally, only 5 percent of CEO positions in real estate are held by women and only 5 percent of presidential positions are held by women. At 18 percent each, the executive leadership positions most widely held by women are "chief financial officer" and "general manager."

Fig. 8: Female Senior Employees in Alternatives as a Proportion of Total Senior Employees by Location and Asset Class

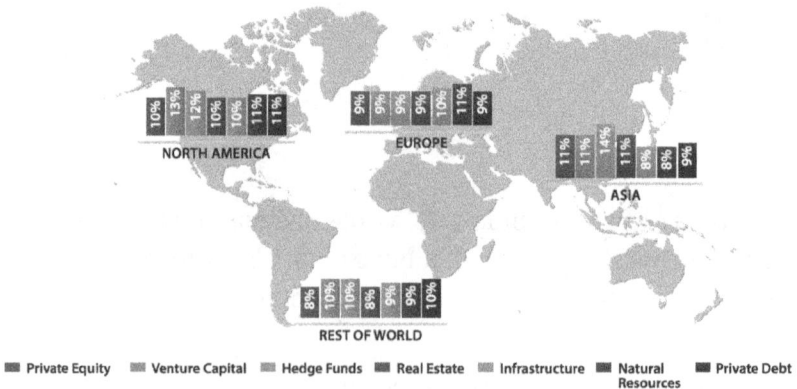

Chart showing women in top-level positions in various industries around the world. Credit: Prequin

"We actually see real estate firms doing slightly better than, say, hedge funds in getting more women through the door and working in those companies," said Amy Bensted, head of hedge fund products at Preqin, who co-authored the 2017 report. "We see higher levels of C-level representation. But the real picture is that females are still grossly under represented within the alternative asset world and there's no real parity in terms of 50-50 split. What you are seeing is that these firms are actually doing better at getting women through the doors in junior levels."

Other respondents to Inman's survey echoed the sentiment that they would like to see more women in leadership positions.

"The leaders are all men," one female-identified respondent wrote in from a leading real estate franchise Iowa. "They have one female broker, but she's not an owner and I've never heard a word from her at company meetings. And, some of the men are silly when it comes to women—one broker wanted to "protect the ladies boobies" and have a mammogram truck visit the office. While the sentiment is there, let's be more grown up about it. And I would question if that's what women actually want from their broker. So, they could incorporate more women. They could listen more. And, if they could put their egos away, that would be great."

Reasons for hope and celebration

In the Inman survey, 55.4 percent of respondents reported that leadership at their company was "very committed to diversity," and another 30.5 percent said it was "somewhat committed to diversity" in the workplace. Only 3.7 percent claimed executives weren't committed at all.

How would you characterize your leaders commitments to workplace diversity?

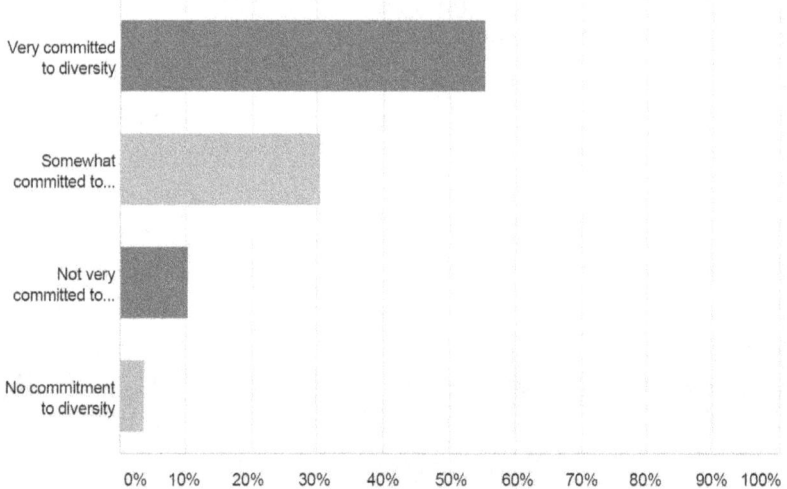

For Kathy Fowler, an Oklahoma City broker associate with Coldwell Banker Select who previously worked in the insurance industry, her transition into real estate was a breath of fresh air—especially with regards to equal footing among her male and female colleagues.

"I was with an independent agent that wrote a lot of commercial and oil and gas insurance, and the females in that industry were expected to be the secretaries and the customer service reps and take care of everything," said Fowler, who also serves as president of the Oklahoma Association of Realtors. "And then the guys went out and wined and dined all the clients."

"In real estate," she added, "I can wine and dine just as much as my male counterparts."

4.

The essential guide for real estate leadership on diversity and hiring

Jotham Sederstrom

Rank-and-file are broadly pleased with leadership

From courage and creativity to communication skills and integrity, real estate professionals largely gave high marks to their leaders, with 49 percent reporting they are "very happy" with senior executives at their companies, another 35 percent saying they are "somewhat happy" and only about 15 percent saying they are "unhappy." Meanwhile, about 40 percent said their leaders frequently rise to challenges in their businesses "very well."

"I'm very happy with our broker," said a Minnesota-based Re/Max agent, one of nearly 800 real estate professional from brokerages big and small surveyed for the Inman poll. "He is providing us the tools to make our job easier and less time consuming. He also listens when you talk."

But among their concerns, many lamented leaders unwilling to adapt to industry changes or new technology—challenges for any executive, to be sure, but perhaps none more so than those in their 50s and 60s, the age group most likely to be in senior positions, according to the survey.

What qualities do you think are most important for good leadership?

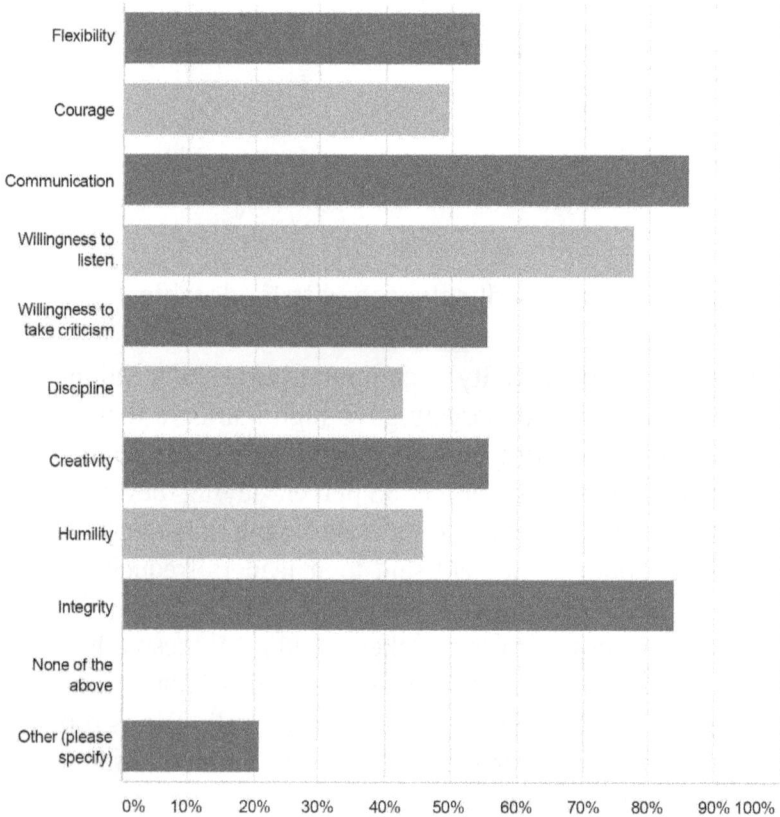

Ageism isn't as big an issue as other industries

However, most leaders were equally willing to hire younger and older brokers alike, with more than 80 percent of real estate professionals saying their leaders supported all age groups. That's an excellent finding compared to other industries such as tech, where age discrimination runs rampant.

Leaders were broadly commended for their commitment to

diversity in the workplace, with 85 percent of real estate professionals giving senior executives positive grades.

Does your leadership support hires of all age groups, or do they tend to favor hires of a certain age group?

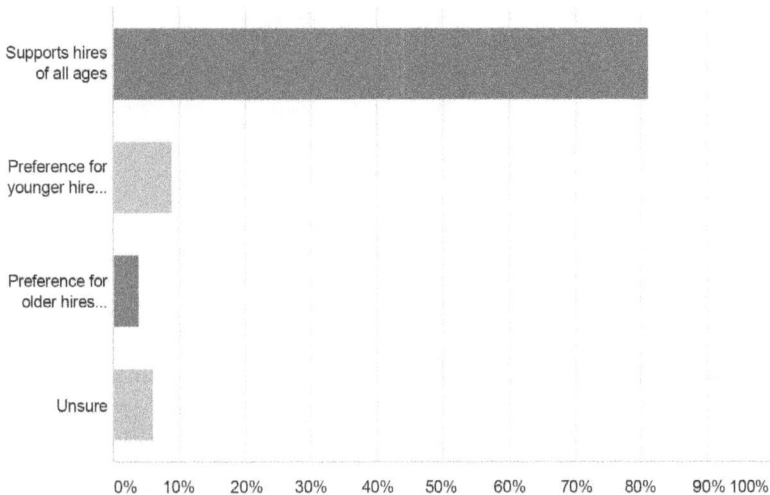

Supports hires of all ages	~80%
Preference for younger hire...	~10%
Preference for older hires...	~5%
Unsure	~8%

(0% 10% 20% 30% 40% 50% 60% 70% 80% 90% 100%)

Specifically, 55.4 percent of respondents reported that leadership
at their company was "very committed to diversity," and another
30.5 percent said it was "somewhat committed to diversity" in the
workplace. Only 3.7 percent claimed executives weren't committed at all.

Yet 40 percent of those polled said that even the most committed
leaders could do more in terms of hiring.

Do your leader(s) know you by your name and what job you do?

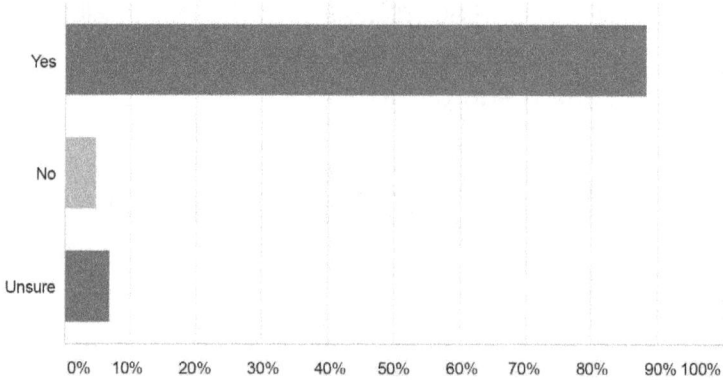

Yes	(bar extending to ~88%)
No	(bar extending to ~5%)
Unsure	(bar extending to ~7%)

0% 10% 20% 30% 40% 50% 60% 70% 80% 90% 100%

Cultural diversity needs work

For Kathy Fowler, a broker associate with Coldwell Banker Select who serves as president of the Oklahoma Association of Realtors and sits on the board of directors for the Oklahoma City Metropolitan Association of Realtors, cultural diversity, while abundant in Oklahoma, is less visible among the upper echelons of the city's realty associations.

"What I'm not seeing represented in Oklahoma as a whole—or at least not in the association world as far as people serving on committees and in leadership and things like that—is cultural diversity," Fowler told Inman News. "And Oklahoma has a very rich, diverse culture, and from my own personal experience with sales transactions, I've experienced the diversity out there, but I haven't seen that diversity involved in the association or in leadership, and that's something I'd like to see us work on, especially on the 50th anniversary of the Fair Housing Act."

Benefits, pay, and other qualms

Benefits and pay were also criticized by real estate professionals, with 31 percent claiming health care is too expensive and 10 percent admitting they don't have insurance. With 85 percent of all real estate agents paid through commissions, according to the poll, about 7 percent of the respondents said they wished they were better compensated.

Others complained of poorly conceived recruitment quotas and an uptick in unqualified or unprofessional agents.

"Signing people because they have a pulse to meet signing quotas irrelevant of their qualifications," griped one Minneapolis Realtor, when asked in the survey how local leaders could improve. "Keeping unprofessional agents on board because they are high producers."

Recruitment-based brokerage models were cited as particularly problematic by Chip Steinmetz, a Re/Max broker-owner in Virginia, who said companies like Coldwell Banker and Keller Williams that offer agents compensation for recruiting new agents are a disservice to clients.

Seinmetz claims that sales agents may not have their clients' best interests at heart if their priority is to recruit the buyer's agent as a new potential colleague.

"Is there a conflict of interest here? Nope," Steinmetz told Inman News in February. "According to all the laws, all the regulations, the NAR code of ethics, there is no conflict, and there is no disclosure requirement. But if your client, the homeowner, were to find out after the house closes that I went to XYZ Realty and that you just capitulated on $5,000 worth of home inspection issues and didn't push back, could somebody reasonably assume that the recruiting activity played a part in that decision? I think it's all in the eyes of the beholder."

5.

The essential guide to real estate leadership on tech and data

Jotham Sederstrom

In Texas, one Coldwell Banker franchise has shifted nearly all of its $150,000 marketing budget from newspaper advertising to social media while retaining a sizable expenditure for staging open houses—an old-school move they still believe to be invaluable for generating business.

At another Coldwell branch in Oklahoma, a top-producing octogenarian couple have thrived as sales agents, in part by embracing the company's Customer Relationship Management tools despite having no computer at home, and refusing to let go of that aging relic: the fax machine.

"What fascinates me personally the most about technology is that we've got these tech tools that automate things for our lives, but at the same time it still comes back to the relationships and relationship-building and keeping in contact with the other humans," said Kathy Fowler, an Oklahoma City broker associate with Coldwell Banker Select, who said her octogenarian colleagues have succeeded through a savvy combination of sales skills both old and new.

From the Midwest to the coasts, in fact, real estate professionals are successfully integrating new technology with traditional sales strategies—even as they call on leaders to more quickly embrace cutting-edge digital platforms, apps and lead generation tools to stay competitive. These and more fascinating results emerged from Inman's inaugural Real Estate Leadership Survey of 787 industry professionals, conducted online in February 2018.

What leaders understand about tech, and what they don't

One thing that was apparent: despite some of the aforementioned examples of how pros are incorporating new technology, leaders have room for improvement.

A total of 39 percent of respondents to Inman's survey said the leadership within their companies is "very techie," while another 46 percent reported that top executives are "somewhat techie." At the same time, 36 percent worried that not adapting quickly to new technology, or a lack of technology altogether, are twin elephants in the room that executives are consistently failing to address.

How technologically literate is your leadership?

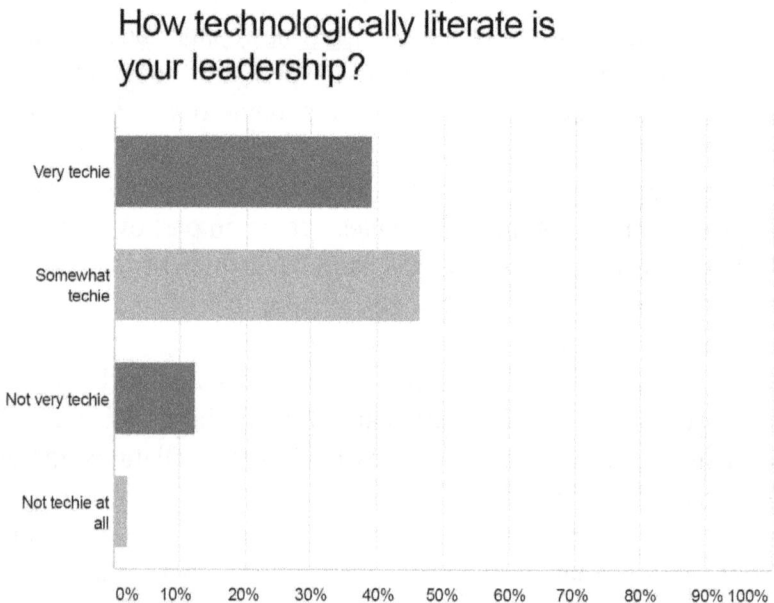

Among the trends most widely embraced by senior executives, social media, digital marketing and lead generation tools are the most prevalent, while more sophisticated innovations—like artificial intelligence, augmented reality and virtual assistants—have yet to take hold despite scattered interest from rank-and-file real estate agents, according to the survey.

However, Google Apps, advanced Customer Relationship Management (CRM) software, and drones were also relatively highly-adopted categories.

Which of the following tech trends or practices has your leadership pushed your organization to adopt?

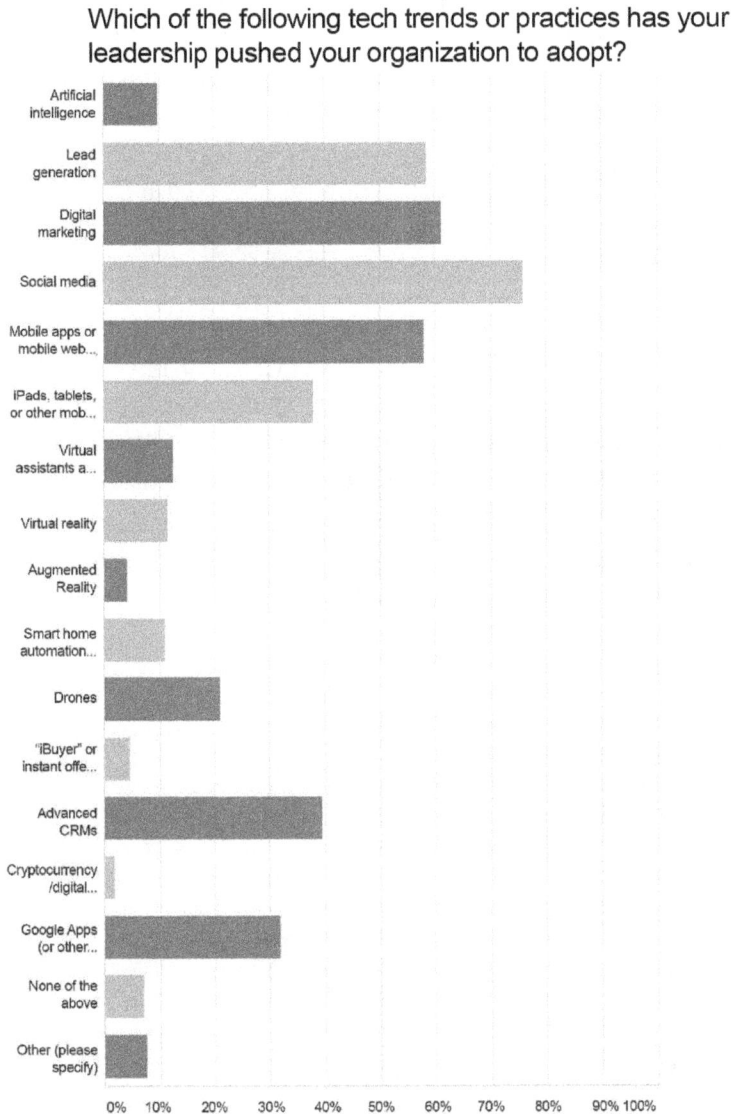

But not everyone in the rank-and-file is thrilled with such a wide embrace of technology, according to the poll. Many agents reported lackluster products and long-term contracts, not to mention a flash-in-the-pan lifecycle for some tools that fall out of favor at lightning speeds.

"Adopting poor technology and then being tied into a long-term contract compounding the poor decision," a Tahoe City, California, Realtor wrote, balking at questionable tech purchases.

"Jumping around to the 'next best thing,'" added a Virginia-based listing agent, citing a gripe among colleagues. "Too many tools and too little intensive instruction on how to use them."

The value of focus

When it came to technology that leaders should be using more of, respondents to Inman's survey were split. Over 24 percent of respondents said they would like to see more use of CRM software. The next highest category of votes was "none of the above," at over 23 percent, followed by artificial intelligence and virtual assistants, at over 21 percent (which should bode well for Keller Williams' recent tack).

What new tools should your company's leadership be using that they don't currently?

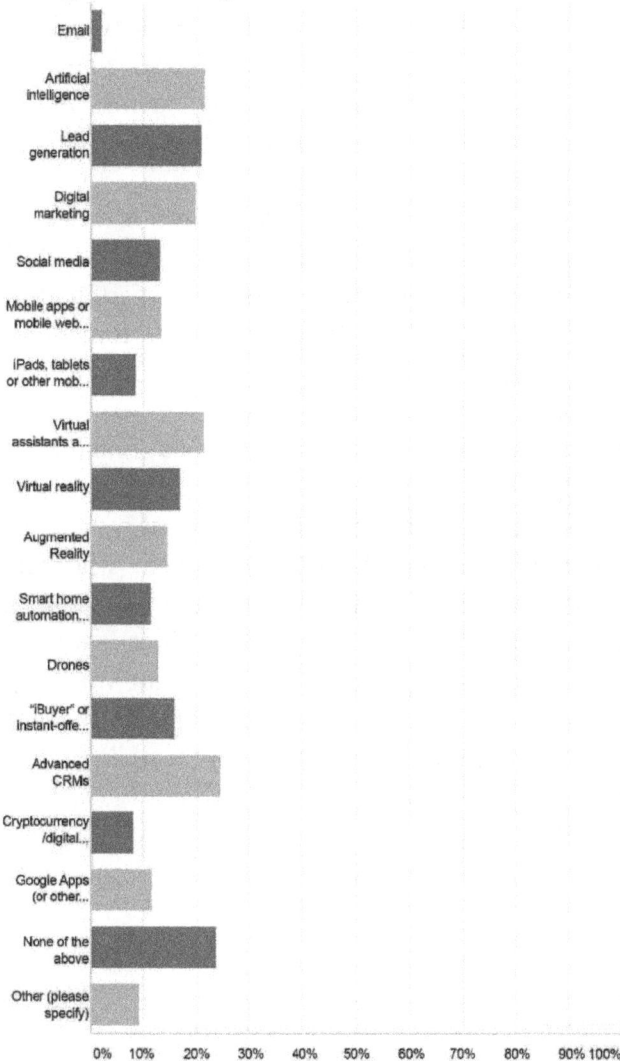

Perhaps somewhat surprisingly, cryptocurrency—which has gotten a lot of buzz in the media (including at Inman) and among the startup community—was one area of technology that most respondents *did not* want to see their leaders using more of. Just over 8 percent of respondents said they wanted to see leaders using more cryptocurrencies (only the category of "email" received fewer votes).

Jake Breen, an associate broker at Berkshire Hathaway Home-Services Utah Properties, said a common misstep among real estate firms is the tendency to spread resources across multiple trends and platforms, rather than focusing on one strategy and executing it with precision.

For years, his team has honed in on high-definition video, regularly producing tours, testimonials and market reports from an in-house studio with the help of a dedicated tech expert, and publishing the content across multiple platforms, he told Inman News late last month. He spends under an hour a day on the origination of data and content for his team's daily videos.

The strategy for real estate leadership, he said, should be to identify the technology that best positions the company's message in front of the consumer—and to hell with the rest of it.

"There's so much noise out there," said Breen, who serves as a broker advisor for REthink, a millennial think tank formed by Berkshire Hathaway HomeServices in 2013. "Leaders need to choose one or two of the top things that they know are working, or that they've seen work for other brokerages, and go all in. There's so much noise out there. Do one, and do it really well."

6.

The essential guide to real estate leadership on social causes

Jotham Sederstrom

Lean into social causes, including disaster relief—but keep your political views to yourself.

In a political climate fraught with anxiety over issues ranging from gun control to civil rights, that's the complicated, albeit conflicted, message to real estate leaders from the 787 industry professionals who responded to Inman's inaugural Leadership in Real Estate survey during a 10-day period in February.

Speak softly but carry a big stick

Nearly 60 percent of responding real estate professionals believe leadership within their companies should support social causes.

They believe the biggest social and economic issues affecting the real estate industry right now are gentrification and affordable housing (40 percent), tax reform (37 percent), government regulations (36 percent), affordable health care (36 percent), untruthful mass media/internet rumors (34 percent) and Realtor/agent safety (26 percent).

Yet, somewhat contradictorily, 66.5 percent also believe that it's unacceptable for their C-level superiors to bring up political, religious or social stances in the workplace or while conducting day-to-day business, according to the Inman survey.

Do you think your leadership should support social causes through your business?

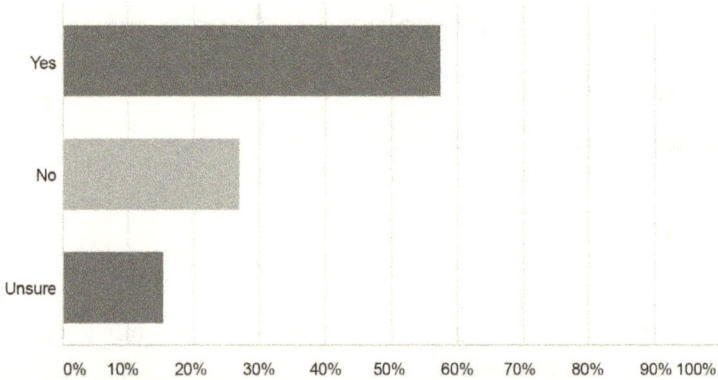

"Like our nation, our brokerage is polarized," wrote one Texas sales associate with Berkshire Hathaway HomeServices, who said leadership at her company should neither endorse political candidates or raise social issues, religious views or political beliefs in public or during work.

Among the real estate respondents, 60 percent said it was either "very important" or "somewhat important" that company leaders reflect the social issues they care about, while about 52 percent said they believe that their employers share their political views. About 13 percent, meanwhile, said it was "not important at all" that their bosses shared their views.

Do you think it's acceptable for leaders to bring up political, religious, or social stances in the workplace or when conducting business?

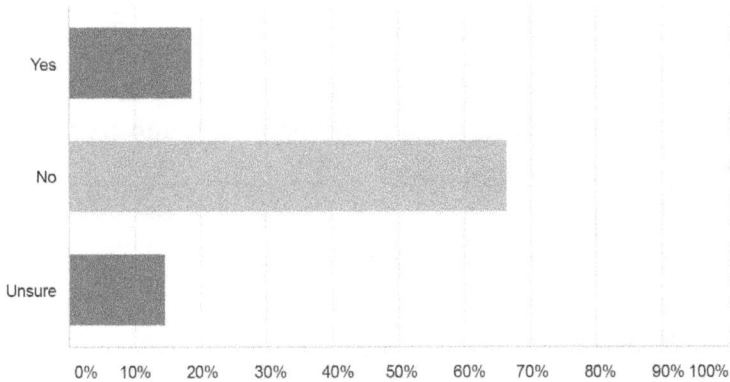

However, a majority of 51 percent of the respondents said real estate leaders should never endorse political candidates, compared to 28 percent who countered that they should endorse them and another 21 percent who said they were "unsure," according to the survey.

"I don't believe that our leadership team should assert their values on us," said one Southern California-based Realtor, who said that industry associations should actively make donations to political candidates and causes. "But, there should be an environment of open discussion."

Helping after disasters

There was some broad unity to be found among Inman's Leadership Survey respondents, especially with regards to assistance in the wake of natural disasters.

An overwhelming majority voiced support for philanthropical work and causes meant to "improve society," including aid for natural disasters such as wildfires that broke out across California in December and hurricanes last summer in Texas, Florida and Puerto

Rico. To be sure, about 60 percent of real estate professionals nationwide said their company leadership had offered aid or assistance in response to a natural disaster, while only about 11 percent claimed their employers had donated nothing to victims of natural disasters.

Does your leadership do enough to offer assistance or aid in response to natural disasters?

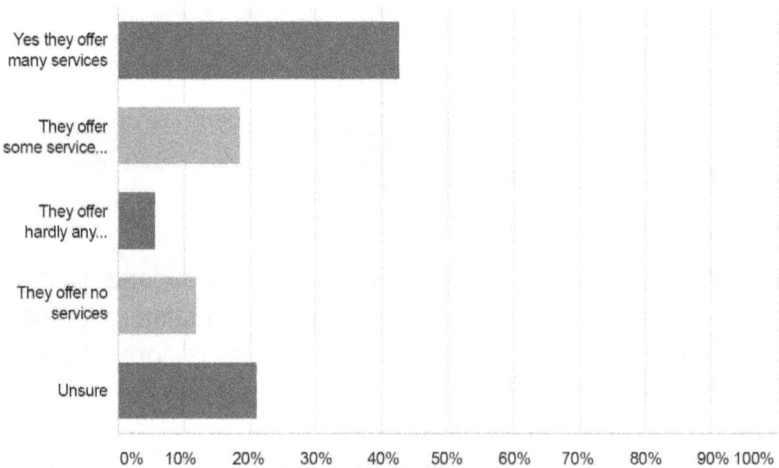

In August and September, when Hurricane Harvey tore through the Gulf Coast, Katie Ruffino and her colleagues at Coldwell Banker Ag-Town Realtors in College Station, Texas, used a company moving van to haul diapers and dog food to those hardest hit in Houston and elsewhere. And when members of the Coast Guard and Navy were stranded at the height of the storm, Ruffino, the lead buyer's agent for the brokerage, helped feed some 400 of the men.

"They were hubbed here, and they were sent with no food, no anything, and so the Realtors here started a whole sign-up," recalled Ruffino, who told Inman News that her team sold about 200 residential units last year. "At one point there were 400 guys from Arkansas that came over actually to help us, and we fed them breakfast, lunch and dinner for three weeks."

"They were saving lives," she added. "Of course we were going to help."

What are the biggest social and economic issues affecting the real estate industry right now?

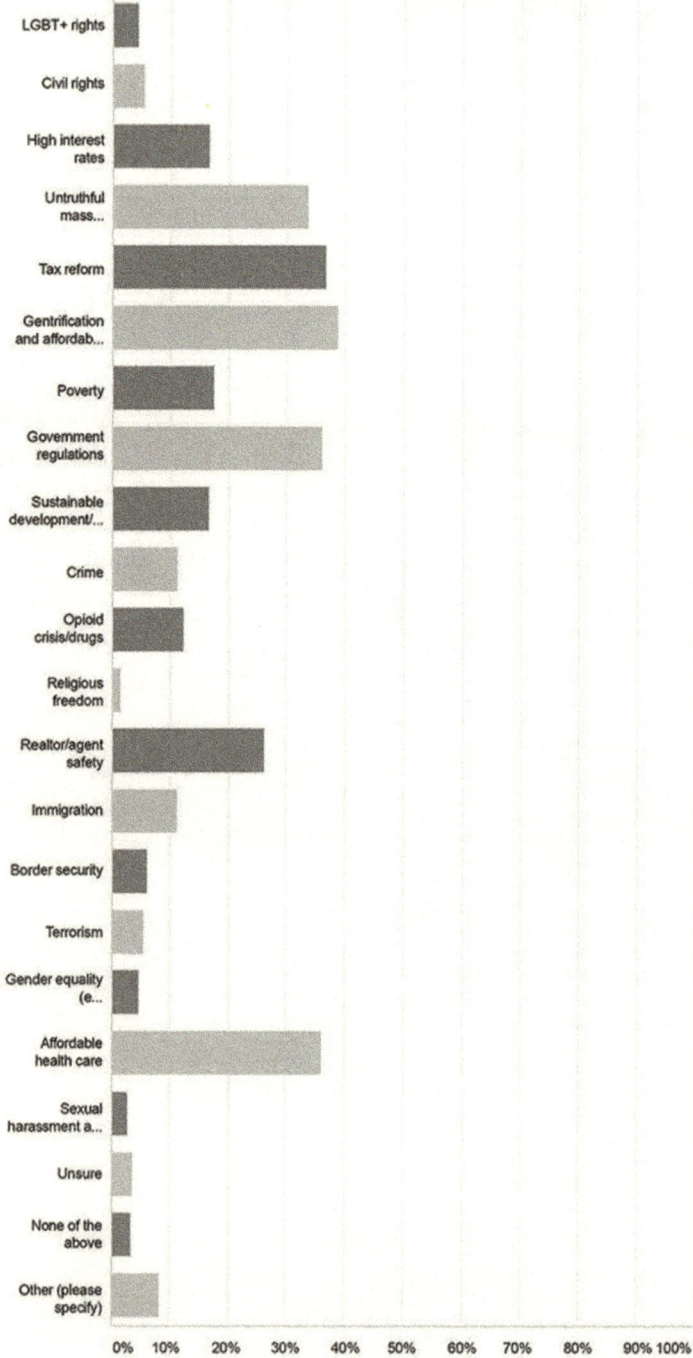

What leaders need to weigh

The debate over politics comes as some of the industry's most visible leaders publicly wrestle with the pros and cons of taking a political stance in a deeply divided country. In January at Inman Connect NYC 2018, Robert Reffkin, the outspoken Compass CEO, and Glenn Kelman, the CEO of publicly traded Redfin, weighed in on the benefits and drawbacks of speaking out politically.

Kelman said that beyond the threat to Redfin's bottom line, speaking out on social causes runs the risk of alienating employees. Nonetheless, he and fellow Redfin executive level felt the need on multiple occasions to speak out in the age of Trump—once on immigration-related matters following a temporary travel ban last year, and another time, in a private letter, to then-North Carolina Gov. Pat McCrory following the enactment of the state's so-called bathroom ban.

"I just have to ask myself, I have to remember, there are employees at Redfin who voted for Donald Trump, there are employees who voted for Hillary Clinton, and they all have helped build the platform that I stand on," Kelman said at the Inman Connect conference in January." And if I use that platform to espouse opinions that they don't support, what am I doing?"

7.

Transparency will radically alter our industry's leadership

Sam DeBord

Inman is asking the industry what the future of real estate leadership looks like. While much of that conversation will focus on who future leaders will be, the most fascinating aspect may be our increasingly transparent environment, which will force leaders to change the way they do business. For those relying on traditional tactics to stay in power, the outlook is bleak.

Through new media and ever-growing access to data, transparency in the real estate industry is driving the massive changes we're seeing in business models and industry power players. Billions of dollars are being invested in the brokerage world, as investors and technologists find ways to engage an informed consumer pool and snatch profits from traditional businesses.

Tomorrow's leaders will strive to give customers greater access and insights through our data, and run their organizations with greater visibility and accountability in this new environment.

Proprietary knowledge as leverage

Knowing more than your customer has been the leverage that many traditional companies used to maintain profits in the past. From individual agents to the industry's largest organizations, proprietary knowledge was power. That advantage is vanishing for many today.

While information-savvy companies are building new and fascinating ways to leverage data, some in the traditional industry are trying to build bigger blinders. Customers, on the other hand—whether they're buyers, sellers, agents or brokers—are demanding transparency and clarity in their business decisions.

The biggest stories in real estate today bear out this transition. Competitors or not, their recent successes have to be recognized and considered.

Redfin advertises its commission rates, its agent salaries, even its performance metrics, to the public. Compass's six-figure onboarding checks, a brokerage tactic that would have been hush-hush in the recent past, is today's open recruiting tool. Low-cost brokerages and franchisors like HomeSmart and NextHome have visibility like no midsize company would have had in the past, and their straightforward, concise pitches are garnering headcounts.

Hanging on

Contrast that with a traditional brokerage whose profits rely upon paying minuscule commission splits to information-deficient agents, while offering "friends and family" deals to favorites. Hold it up against the brokerage that loses money on its transactions because it can't pull the plug on its 40-year-old compensations plans, but keeps the lights on through junk fees and ancillary "profit centers" while hoping its agents are too busy to see the fat in the system.

The traditional brokerage model, like much of organized real estate, is at a crossroads, and its leaders will either be open to this new business environment or their businesses will stagnate.

A traditional mindset

It's not just the brokerage world that's held back by tradition. "Traditional" real estate is a franchisor that treats every customer relationship like a secret one-off negotiation. It's a service business granting sweetheart deals that promote some of its customers at the expense of others, all the while hoping that these customers are informationally siloed and never compare notes.

"Traditional" is a Realtor board that takes semi-annual international boondoggles on its members' dime with no metrics for the return on investment or accountability measures. It's a multiple listing service (MLS) that intentionally prohibits its brokers from using their own data as a tactic to inhibit consolidation. It's an association that practices a "Keep others out" philosophy in executive session, even as its brokers are calling for more cooperation and transparency.

These traditional ways of leading our organizations, which used to be contained in closed-door meetings and whispers between friends, are being exposed. They're discussed openly in public forums. They're shared between ever more closely networked professionals across geographies.

They have no future in a transparent real estate world

There is hope for current leaders if they accept this atmosphere of high visibility and rapid change, and seek to inspire success and responsibility in an environment that will require both. Moves toward a philosophy of openness are being seen even in the industry's most long-standing organizations.

The manner in which the National Association of Realtors (NAR) recently shuttered AMP illustrated just how this "leadership in the sunlight" must be carried out. CEO Bob Goldberg's blunt comments on the financial and operational inefficiencies of the project were unprecedented, unexpected and refreshing to a large swath of membership which has been anxious about the trade organization's fiscal operations.

Though some small and mid-sized MLSs are undoubtedly disappointed at the loss of the opportunity AMP promised, the openness of the explanation and the focus on fiscal responsibility was thoroughly appreciated by most.

When transparency chooses you

Of course, transparency can be initiated by an organization within itself, but it also can come as a directive through regulation. The Federal Trade Commission (FTC) and U.S. Department of Justice (DOJ) will reportedly investigate real estate competition in the coming months.

The questions will surround the expiration of the DOJ/NAR VOW settlement—in essence, an inquiry into whether the industry is appropriately allowing access to real estate data for all participants.

"Think tanks" have proposed regulating listing databases in the belief that MLSs somehow restrict visibility of listings. Though sometimes thoroughly misguided, never doubt the government's interest in bringing greater transparency to a marketplace. It's the dream of many well-intentioned, yet often underinformed bureaucrats, and it's the duty of the industry to build a transparent and competitive marketplace before someone else decides to "fix" it for us.

That process is already in place through many efforts, not the least of which is the Broker Public Portal (BPP). Regulators need to look no further than this volunteer conglomeration of leaders that brings thousands of brokers, over 100 MLSs and over 800,000 agents' listings together for public consumption. Its existence is evidence that transparency is now a driving goal for some of the industry. Today's leaders would do well to begin their paths toward transparency by joining in.

The skeletons in the closet will be exposed

This transparency coming to real estate will affect how we work with our current customers, as well as exposing our historical business practices. Scrutiny is growing over the way leaders conduct themselves across every industry.

Employees write tell-all stories about maniacal executives that go viral and often result in leadership being forced out. The movement to expose sexual harassment in the workplace is a freight train bearing down on every C-suite in the world. The HR department's secret files and the corporate hush money checks won't keep bad behavior in the shadows forever. Leaders must conduct business like their corporate files will eventually be exposed because, as is becoming painfully clear, very little is truly secret or secure. Even the communications of the highest offices in the land find their way into the public eye.

Whether you cheer or fear this future, it's coming.

This progression toward transparency will be good for the real estate industry, though it will be a painful process for many. Our businesses do not exist in a vacuum. The knowledge-empowered consumer, and the public, will demand that we operate transparently and with accountability. There's no better time than today for our leaders to embrace those values as fundamental to the success of our organizations.

8.

How to create a brokerage culture of inclusion

Elizabeth Ann Stribling-Kivlan with Gill South

Elizabeth Ann Stribling-Kivlan

"You can fake a lot of things in this world, but you can't fake culture," said Elizabeth Ann Stribling-Kivlan, president of leading luxury New York City brokerage Stribling & Associates, in an interview with Inman.

Stribling-Kivlan was 10-months-old when her mother, Elizabeth F. Stribling, launched Stribling & Associates 37 years ago. Now, as co-owner of the brokerage with her mother, Stribling-Kivlan has grown the company to include more than 300 agents in four offices across Manhattan and Brooklyn—and she's done so on the pillars of inclusion, community and independence.

In practice that means fostering open-door, informal communication (Stribling-Kivlan often texts with her agents), and developing clear procedures for agents for what to do if they ever feel uncomfortable or unsafe.

"I know everyone who works for me," she said. "If you are

afraid to talk to me because I'm head of the firm, I'm doing something wrong. I sit with my agents, I'm always around." Stribling-Kivlan also likes to give equal attention to all agents, rather than focusing on top producers.

According to Stribling-Kivlan, as much as she likes to make herself personally available, it makes sense to have a number of managers in your brokerage whom agents and staff know they can reach out to. With the dawn of the #MeToo movement and raised awareness of sexual harassment in the workplace, policies for reporting acts of misconduct are more important than ever, in real estate and across industries, said Stribling-Kivlan.

The company also has an annual management meeting in which the company discusses its position on codes of behavior, making sure they are creating a healthy culture and an inclusive environment. Agents and staff also go through diversity training.

"Do people enjoy it? No," said Stribling-Kivlan. "But they learn and often say: 'I didn't know that was our response,'" to this or that issue.

Stribling-Kivlan, who is openly gay and happily married, is very involved in several LGBTQ groups. She recently changed the wording in the company's agent and employee handbook to become gender neutral, changing references from "he/she" to "they." She made this decision because she didn't want to make assumptions about anyone, including clients.

"Just because you can't see something doesn't mean it doesn't exist—I want them [everyone in the company] to feel like they have a safe space here which they may not have at home," she said.

For her 330 agents, it's about being "more enlightened," said Stribling-Kivlan. "You are selling and leasing to an entire population, not just to a one-gendered person."

Ken Scheff, manager of the brokerage's Uptown office, sees commonalities between the modern Elizabeth Ann, known as "EA," in the office and the more proper but also kind, Elizabeth, her mother.

"Neither are interested in a corporate environment, but rather a high ethos," said Scheff. "I think the goal is not to be corporate.

They both love food, the arts and theater as well as the city, architecture and design."

Scheff said there is a "palpable feeling" at Stribling & Associates that there is no parent company hovering, no corporate pressure in the background.

As Stribling-Kivlan puts it: "There are not many of us left—there are very few independents and we truly are independent."

Added Scheff: "There is a very strong sense of trying to do the right thing. It's very broker-centric, there is very little turnover."

Stribling-Kivlan said she wants her agents to wake up and to want to come to work. It's about creating a community, and balancing work and life.

She likes to think the company still has a startup vibe, despite its size and nearly four-decade-long history. Stribling & Associates, which posted $1.6 billion in Manhattan sales volume last year, is third behind top dogs Douglas Elliman and Corcoran Group.

"It's about having fun together, too, that's really important," said Stribling-Kivlan, mentioning an office bowling night coming up in the near future. "We don't have a ping-pong table, but we have everything else I think."

9.

Leadership in real estate: Courage is what we need

Rob Hahn

I've been asked by the good folks at Inman to give some thought to the question of leadership as part of their efforts to revolutionize leadership in real estate. Seeing as how yours truly does not lack for opinions on a variety of topics, and this one in particular, I thought I would happily oblige them.

First, we need to define the term "leadership" because it's important to be precise when discussing ideas and philosophies—Lord only knows when it comes to definitions for "leadership," everybody's got one. And there are so many dimensions to "leadership," that it's a difficult concept to pin down.

So, I'll define leadership in the same logically fallacious, conclusory fashion as does Jimmy Collins, retired President of Chick-fil-A for 33 years:

> *"**A leader is someone who has followers**. If there are no followers, there is no leader. A person may have subordinates, workers, admirers, associates, co-workers, friends and people who report to him or her, a person may have authority over other people, a person may hold an elective office, and a person may influence a large number of people, but **that does not make that person a leader if there are no followers.**"*

The reason I define it this way is to contrast it from *positionship*, which is rampant everywhere, but particularly in real estate.

My current thinking on leadership in real estate is this: More than ever, we need **courage**. The current generation of leaders must be willing and able to ask hard questions and make tough decisions that won't make him or her popular, but will result in saving the real estate industry as we know it.

Let's get into it. Section titles may or may not be taken from George Martin's *A Song of Ice and Fire* series.

A Storm of Swords

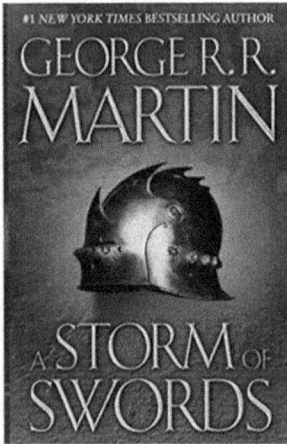

To start, we must agree that there are critical challenges for the industry starting at the cusp of 2020. If we do not, if you believe that everything is hunkydory, that the biggest problem in real estate is Zillow, that there are not fundamental problems that will blow up sooner or later in unpredictable ways—well, then we have nothing to talk about.

If "steady as she goes" is good enough, then by all means, let's have steady as she goes and people who are really good at managing the status quo.

I believe the opposite. I believe there are at least three fundamental problems in real estate that—if left unchecked, if not addressed, if kicked down the road—will blow up and bring about fundamental transformation of the industry with enormous possible negative consequences. They are:

- Agent incompetence
- Lack of broker profitability
- Broken organized real estate

What's more, the three fundamental problems are *interrelated* and *interdependent*.

For example, lack of broker profitability drives headcount-based, recruit-and-retain models, which leads to broken association/MLS models based on membership dues from as many people as possible, which results in widespread and rampant incompetence by agents who are card-carrying, dues-paying Realtors, which in turn degrades the Realtor brand, and so on and so forth.

Left untreated, these problems will result in the outside world imposing solutions on the industry, whether through technology disruption, government action or simple changes in consumer behavior.

In many cases, those solutions will be for the better; in other cases, however, the cure may very well be worse than the disease.

This situation calls for leadership that is strategic, wise, caring, empathetic, and so on and so forth—all of the things that experts and non-experts alike want from their leaders. But above all, leadership today requires *courage*.

When problems are fundamental, tweaking around the edges ain't gonna get it done. And you can't mess with fundamental solutions if you're deathly afraid of offending this person or that person or constantly worried about job security.

A Game of Thrones

Given the fundamental problems, there are some secondary issues as well. One of the most significant is the plethora of people practicing positionship and a dearth of people practicing leadership.

What is "positionship"? There are, once again, many definitions, but I like this one from John Maxwell (paraphrased): **people follow you because they have to**. You're the CEO, so your subordinates do as you say, but they don't follow you in any significant sense of the term. You've been elected president, so the by-laws grant you certain powers, which you're not shy about exercising. But

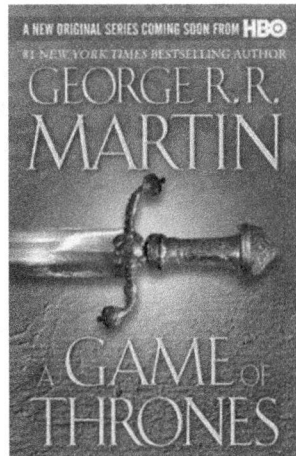

you've got no followers, and once your term is over, you'll disappear like sea foam into the ocean waves.

In the brokerage world, there are tens of thousands of owners/ CEO/brokers, and under them, there are even more tens of thousands of mid-level managers who toe the company line and try nothing extraordinary because they want to keep their jobs, keep their titles, keep their positions.

The brokers don't practice leadership because they're beholden to certain top producing agents and keeping them fat and happy is their top priority.

In the MLS and association world, positionship is the norm rather than the exception. The constant revolving door of "leadership" at local, state and national levels means a president is here one year, gone the next.

The association executive or the MLS CEO understands that his or her job depends on politics and keeping the board fat and happy, and so they take no risks they don't have to. Why rock the boat?

The power games, the intrigues, the perceived slights and offenses, the desperate need for validation by some unknown crowd of "insiders" who will or won't nominate you for some position or another—these things are the daily realities of organized real estate in the 21st century.

Yet, there are leaders—men and women whom others follow without having to, simply because they inspire and educate in some way. If the industry is lucky, those few leaders will also get the position, which gives them the power to do something about pressing issues.

If we're not, the leaders get overlooked and silenced by those interested in the position and the power for their own sake.

A Clash of Kings

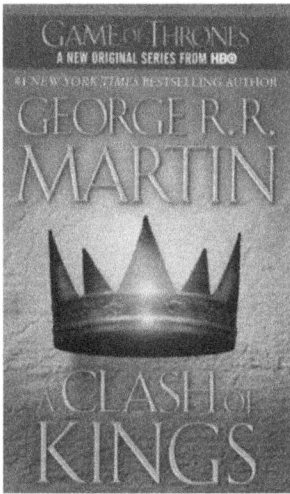

What then do we need from our leaders? I have said above, it is courage above all, right now, at this time.

The fundamental problems facing the industry require fundamental solutions. That means destroying that which does not work any longer. That means questioning where we're headed and why. That means upsetting the comfortable arrangements that have profited so many for so long. Naturally, those who depend on the status quo for their jobs, their positions, and their status will not simply *let things go*. It doesn't work that way.

We need people who are comfortable in their own skin, who do not need positions to give them followers, who do not need the approval of others for their self-esteem and who do not rely on the status quo for their livelihoods.

Then we need them to step up, with courage (which does not mean the absence of fear) to change what must be changed, to destroy what must be destroyed and to build what must be built.

We might call such people kings and queens arising. They will assuredly clash with the old guard of kings and queens. The latter will have power, money, influence, positions, titles and even companies.

But the former will have truth and reality on their side, if they would only speak the truth and act on the reality of today instead of the faded illusions of the past.

This has to be done. There will be conflict, and it will be unpleasant, no doubt. But it must happen if we're to have a chance.

Otherwise …

A Feast for Crows

The future looks grim for the real estate industry. The following is merely a list of things that we already know about.

God only knows what else is being cooked up in some garage in Silicon Valley or in some backroom in some state capitol somewhere that we have no idea about at all.

- DOJ and FTC hearing to review the state of competition in real estate, with a particular focus on how real estate data is used or not used.

- New models of buying/selling homes including Opendoor, OfferPad and Knock

- New brokerage models from Redfin to Purplebricks to pay-you-to-list-your-home (you read that right)

- The end to self-regulation of the industry (already happened in British Columbia, Canada)

- The continual rise of private listing networks

- Challenges to independent contractor status of real estate agents

- Challenges to licensing for real estate brokers and agents

- Questions on whether commission sharing is desirable for consumers or not

- Greater difficulty in keeping banks out of real estate

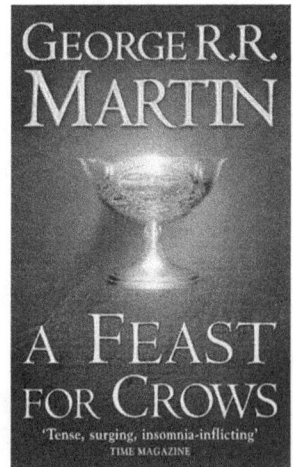

Some of the changes that will be forced on us from the outside may be positive overall. But many won't be, and once we have lost control, well, we have lost control.

None of us can predict what that looks like, except that it will be *exponentially more difficult to regain control once lost than it is to fix what's broken while we have some control.*

A Dream of Spring

A Dream of Spring

So at this time in the industry's history, what is needed above all are leaders who have the *courage* to ask hard questions and make tough decisions.

Several years back, Stefan Swanepoel wrote a book called *Surviving Your Serengeti.* I reviewed it in 2011, and in that book review, I wrote:

"The natural cynic, like yours truly, might have fun with some of the lessons. For example, the wildebeest embodies endurance, and Stefan spends quite a few pages pointing out that the wildebeest's journey is fraught with peril, with no guarantees of survival, but exults in the fact that the wildebeest overcame all of those dangers to become the most populous animal on the Serengeti. I couldn't help but think, however, that the species as a whole may endure, but individual wildebeests get eaten. Thousands of them."

If the real estate industry is to survive, the leaders will have to make decisions that result in thousands of casualties. Companies will go bankrupt. People will lose their jobs. Whole organizations may fail, and even whole sub-industries disappear. But the herd, the real estate industry as we know it, will survive.

Those are tough decisions for tough men and women.

These leaders may be in positions of power already. Or they might be on the outside looking in. But they will all have followers, and few will have comfortable words of calm and peace and everything's gonna be all right.

Because in our time, the challenges confronting us, do not lend themselves easily to messages of peace and comfort and go along to get along. It will take far more than positionship, which can be taken away by a board of directors, by a committee, by some institution or another, to get the industry from here to there.

We can only hope to see these leaders emerge and start to lead.

Because the alternative to hard questions, tough decisions and choices that nobody wants to make is a happy-faced, comfortable, bump-free ride into irrelevance and extinction.

Could such leaders emerge in this social-media-addled, popularity-above-all, politically correct and socially divided Instagram world of ours?

I don't know the answer, but I'm hoping for their emergence and ultimate triumph, I dream of spring. I dream of a springtime of a new revitalized real estate industry that fulfills its patriotic duty and civic responsibility as laid out for us over a hundred years ago by our forefathers, that cares for and serves consumers as they deserve and that elevates the industry to something beyond ordinary commerce.

Come what may, that's a dream worth having.

10.

Leadership Lens: It's easier to be the agent of change

Glenn Kelman

Glenn Kelman

We recently sat down with Glenn Kelman, the president and CEO at Redfin. Prior to joining Redfin, he was a co-founder of Plumtree Software, a Sequoia-backed, publicly traded company that created the enterprise portal software market. Glenn was raised in Seattle and graduated from the University of California, Berkeley. He is a regular contributor to the Redfin blog and Twitter.

As a leader, what keeps you up at night?

Just that we do the most basic things very well, like showing up to a home tour or a listing consultation well prepared, and that we put our customers' interests first. As businesses grow, we tend to serve ourselves instead of our original mission to help people and then lose our way. Redfin has to stay true to its calling.

If you could change one thing in real estate, what would it be?

That we use the institutions we already have for working together to modernize how we share data, so that agents get a better deal when sharing their listings, and the industry makes it easier to schedule home tours, prepare offers and sell houses online. Brokers could make more money if we were all committed to labor-saving technologies.

How have your expectations of your management team changed over the past two years?

I delegate more strategic projects. For example, our chief technology officer, Bridget Frey, ran the process for setting Redfin's goals this quarter. The leader of our Texas business, Jason Aleem, figured out how we wanted to improve our service this year, and how many agents we'd have to hire to do it. We've become more explicit in recognizing that the ability to resolve ambiguity is what separates an executive from, say, a project leader.

How do you keep your team competitive?

Mostly, by hiring folks with a big motor. If someone wasn't born that way, I won't make her that way. Then you have to run the business by the numbers. It's so easy to lie to yourself. If we didn't agree on how to keep score in a game of Scrabble, everyone would say he or she won. Redfin has failed more than most brokerages, but we've been able to recover from those failures in part because everyone can immediately see a failure as such.

With so much disruption in real estate, what's your best advice for managing change?

I once heard a bank robber on a radio show talk about how he calmed himself before a heist. He'd pull the car over, and, his hands still shaking on the wheel, he'd remind himself that he was the perpetrator, not the victim. Then feeling calm again, he'd rob the bank. I don't recommend robbing banks, but I think it's easier to be the agent of change than to respond to change. Every major brokerage has something it can do better than any other, based on its market share, culture, local presence or technical abilities. How can you use that to be the perpetrator of change?

One more analogy: as a soccer player, I used to try to trap a punted ball dead to my feet, so I could then decide what to do with it. If you've ever tried to absorb the energy of a ball kicked 50 yards through the air, you know this is impossible. Later I learned it was much easier to redirect it in the direction I wanted to go. It would carom 10 yards away from me, but because I was the one who kicked it, I was already running toward it. Change is the same way. You can't stop it. You don't even want to. Just channel it in your direction.

11.

Leadership Lens: Robert Reffkin on tackling hard problems

Robert Reffkin

Robert Reffkin

Robert Reffkin is the founder and CEO of Compass. Combining the country's top agents, proprietary market insights and integrated mobile and web technologies, technology-driven real estate platform Compass is dedicated to creating a seamless and intelligent homebuying, selling and renting experience.

Since founding the company in 2013, Compass has raised $775 million in investor capital and has expanded to every major city across the country, including New York City, Los Angeles, Chicago, Dallas, San Francisco, Boston, Washington, D.C., Miami, and Aspen. We recently sat down with Robert to pick his brain about the future of real estate leadership.

As a leader, what keeps you up at night?

I wake up in the morning and go to bed at night thinking about what more I and Compass can do to help our agents grow their business. My wife would probably tell you that I don't sleep enough, so I guess you could argue that that's what keeps me up at night.

I also think about the future we're creating. For our children, for our agents, for our employees. Do our agents feel more supported by our technology and marketing than they ever knew possible? Does every Compass employee feel like they are doing the most meaningful work of their career? What more can we do to help everyone find their place in the world through a better real estate experience for agents and their clients?

If you could change one thing in real estate, what would it be?

If I could change one thing about real estate it would be that the industry would provide access to affordable healthcare for agents and their families.

How have your expectations of your management team changed over the past two years?

A few thoughts here:

1. I want everyone on our leadership team to focus more on maximizing their strengths and less on trying to turn their weaknesses into strengths. The upside of focusing on the things someone is very good at is much greater than the upside of being marginally better at things someone is weak at.

2. I want everyone at Compass focused on results. Not activities, but actual, measurable results that tie to our goal of helping agents make more money. This is a big focus for us this year. Everyone on our team at all levels works very hard, and I want to ensure everyone's work has real business impact.

I've seen projects that are well intended, but don't have any measurable impact. I want everyone focused on work that drives our agents' businesses in a very direct way.

3. I expect our managers to be the best managers. The data shows that the quality of a person's manager impacts their job satisfaction by 70 percent. That's a huge risk and an opportunity, so

we need to make sure all of our managers are the best in the world, and that's a priority for us in 2018.

How do you keep your team competitive?

I believe that in order to give yourself the energy and drive to do big things, you have to feel like your work is worth doing. So, we make sure that we're offering our people big problems to solve. By bringing everything we do back to our mission—to help everyone find their place in the world—we find no shortage of exciting, hard problems to tackle.

On a tactical level, we set aspirational objectives for the company, with measurable results for what success will look like at the end of the year. Then, all of our teams create their own results tied to our aspirational objectives. We share those across the company and give regular updates.

We believe in total transparency, so if I'm not meeting my results, the whole company will know it. It's less about competition, and more about creating the space to learn the lessons we need to learn in order to constantly improve, and opening up opportunities for collaboration.

With so much disruption in real estate, what's your best advice for managing change?

Real estate agents are entrepreneurs. They are agile and resilient. I think the best agents will manage this change the same way they've managed every change before this: by embracing it. We should follow their lead.

12.

Leadership Lens: Change doesn't occur because everyone wants it

David Charron

David Charron

David Charron is currently the chief strategy officer and director for Bright MLS. Bright facilitated $91 billion in residential real estate transactions in 2017. He is president of MRIS and chairs its investment committee. David serves as chair of the National Broker Portal/Homesnap and is the 2018 president of the Council of MLSs (CMLS).

He has served with Midwest Real Estate Data (MRED) as its first strategic manager. He served as a board member of the Realtors Federal Credit Union as well as the NAR MLS Policy Committee. He is a founding member of COVE, an industry think tank comprised of large MLSs.

We recently spent some time with David to pick his brain about the future of real estate leadership.

As a leader, what keeps you up at night?

The horizon and its possibilities. Conversely, people anchored in the past who invariably stand in the way, protectors vs enablers and artificial barriers. As you can see, I work at both ends of the spectrum and don't get as much sleep as I would like!

If you could change one thing in real estate, what would it be?

That we would spend more time challenging one's point of view and less time challenging his or her integrity. Words matter.

How have your expectations of your management team changed over the past two years?

Even greater emphasis on whatever they/we do—it must be essential, timely and measurable.

How do you keep your team competitive?

One element of staying competitive is to study the competition. Channeling and paraphrasing Indira Noori CEO of PepsiCo and the "Queen of (soda) Pop": "Think first about how competitors can help you learn more about your business. Worry less about how they will kill it."

With so much disruption in real estate, what's your best advice for managing change?

Change doesn't occur because everyone wants it. It occurs because a need has been identified and that need will be met. Change is loyal to no one. Change only sees the opportunity to impact the status quo. As a result, go ahead and innovate (carefully) on your base. Importantly, do it before someone else does.

13.

Leadership Lens: Why aren't we harnessing technology?

Joe Rand

We recently sat down with Joe Rand, Managing Partner of Better Homes and Gardens Rand Realty, one of the largest family-owned real estate brokerages in the country, to get his thoughts on the current state of real estate leadership. In 2015, Better Homes and Gardens Rand Realty participated in over $1.8 billion in real estate transactions, becoming one of the top 100 real estate companies in the country.

Joe Rand

As a leader, what keeps you up at night?

I wish I could quote Mad Dog Mattis and say something like, "I keep other people up at night," but I don't think that's true. As a broker, I'm always worried about keeping the faith of the agents who have associated with us. We are constantly refining our value proposition for them. But it's even more important that we continue to inspire them, and keep their confidence that we are the best partners to help them build their real estate careers. So we're always looking for ways to keep that edge, to stay ahead of our competition.

If you could change one thing in real estate, what would it be?

I would change the focus of our industry from thinking of ourselves as a sales industry and more like a professional services industry. I just think that our mindset is all wrong, that it makes agents short-sighted and obsessed with short-term lead generation rather than developing long-term relationships.

And that mindset affects everything, from our hiring practices to training and education to where we put our innovative resources and energies. Everything is about generating leads, not improving the client experience. That's why we're vulnerable to disruption, because we don't have the kind of consistent value proposition that fends off competitive models.

How have your expectations of your management team changed over the past two years?

We expect too much of our managers. They need to do everything: recruiting, coaching, managing, administration, culture maintenance, etc. I think what we've done differently recently is enhance our accountability for managers to ensure that they're following our systems. We have, for example, a weekly call with each region where we review activities for the week and preview the coming week.

With 30 offices, it's tough to stay on top of everyone, but that's one way we're trying. Also, we changed our compensation system to give managers an incentive to drive profitability, recruiting, and affiliate conversion—their bonus is based on an interplay of all three metrics, a change from our old system where it was simply based on office profitability. Now, they can boost that bonus by hitting goals for recruiting and affiliate conversion as well.

How do you keep your team competitive?

We are constantly training everyone and creating new systems for refining our operations. We're big believers in trying to make systems easier for agents and managers, so we're always looking for inefficiencies that are holding us back.

With so much disruption in real estate, what's your best advice for managing change?

We need to embrace change, harness that energy for our own benefit.

For example, Opendoor is a potential disruptor, but the traditional real estate industry already has 1.2 million boots on the ground (actually 2.4 million boots, assuming everyone has two feet) of people who know their local markets and could source opportunities for competing Instant Buyer programs.

Rather than put our head in the sand, or shake our fists, we should be trying to turn Opendoor into MySpace. And that's just one example. Our industry has smart leaders and a lot of ways to get financial backing—why aren't we the ones who are harnessing technology to drive change?

14.

Leadership Lens: Higher standards, now more than ever

Vanessa Bergmark

Vanessa Bergmark

Vanessa Bergmark is the CEO/Owner of Red Oak Realty in Oakland, California. Located in the San Francisco Bay Area, the Red Oak Opportunity Foundation partners with local non-profits to make a difference, and has distributed grants totaling more than $1,170,000.

We recently sat down with Vanessa to ask her views on the current state of real estate leadership.

As a leader, what keeps you up at night?

Staying competitive. Staying sharp.

I am thrilled with where my company is, however, I am concerned with getting complacent and missing opportunities. There's a fine line between having gratitude for what you have and just maintaining where you are at, while striving for growth and progress.

Worth noting that if it truly does keep me up at night, I get *out* of bed and deal with it. Tim Ferris teaches about fear setting rather than goal setting and on many of those sleepless nights, I fear set.

If you could change one thing in real estate, what would it be?

The reputation. I am proud of what I do. I work hard, and I know how hard my agents and staff work for our clients. It's always a bit of a punch in the gut when I am at a dinner party, a retreat, a backyard BBQ or my kid's school when somebody asks, "What do you do?" and I see an actual grimace when I respond.

There's a lot of consumer mistrust and overall aggravation about the way real estate transactions are handled and, ultimately, what agents are paid. I'd love to commit more of my time in changing the consumer image of the entire profession. I think it would have a positive effect on the experience during the transaction if consumers entered the process with higher trust and better expectations of the process and more transparency.

I'd love to see a smile when I say what I do.

How have your expectations of your management team changed over the past 2 years?

I hold my team to higher standards now more so than I ever have. As my team has changed over the years, any new hires are also held to a higher standard. They have to be informed not only on our local market, but our industry. They have to stay not only up to date on tech and product offerings, but informed on what is up and coming in the near future and how it may apply to and benefit our business.

They have to have leadership qualities themselves, make decisions without me, stay on track of projects and be responsible for managing crisis and handling difficult agent and consumer related issues.

I expect them to move swiftly with competitive pace and confront issues quickly. No languishing allowed. I also hold them to the same standard I hold myself. Nothing I ask of anyone is something I wouldn't do, and they often remark on this. Of note, my management team has changed from almost all men to entirely women in the past 2 years.

How do you keep your team competitive?

I educate them on the industry. I challenge them on what they read, watch and talk about. I hold a high standard of how they treat one another and confront conflict openly. We all work with coaches and consultants on short term projects and long term goals and culture.

We have started to set company goals that the entire staff team—16 women—will benefit from financially if we reach. We openly challenge as well as support each other.

With so much disruption in real estate, what's your best advice for managing change?

Embrace it. Have fun with it. Look at it as an opportunity to get rid of things you tolerated or disliked—not just as the annoyance of constantly having to improve. Some things need to change; understanding why the change is at hand and comprehending why it is happening and how it will benefit us makes the process of changing less adversarial.

Frankly, I've never really had a problem with change, and when others see you getting curious and inspired by it, change can get contagious and exciting.

15.

Leadership Lens: Hire brilliant and competitive people

Jed Carlson

Jed Carlson is the chief executive officer of Adwerx, a digital marketing platform for real estate. Jed believes real estate agents should get the same tools as rock stars, literally.

Jed is obsessed with taking on the digital challenges that face small businesses, and building scalable, simple and affordable products to solve them. He is also an active angel investor, mentor and advisor to over ten tech startups. And he's a frequent speaker and panelist at conferences on technology and digital marketing.

We recently got the opportunity to sit down with Jed and pick his brain about where real estate leadership is headed in 2018.

As a leader, what keeps you up at night?

If I were to breakdown my sleepless hours, I would say 25 percent are spent thinking about internal alignment—is everyone pulling on the same rope, and if not, how do we fix that?

Twenty-five percent is big picture strategy—have we identified the right opportunities to pursue, and do we have a solid plan to pursue them?

Another 25 percent is spent thinking about people—our team, our customers and partners, our shareholders.

And the last 25 percent is probably spent on broader topics about the industry, the economy, humanity, etc.

If you could change one thing in real estate, what would it be?

If I could wave a magic wand to standardize data and make it open and available to all, I would absolutely do that. Advertising automation (what we do) requires data as the input.

Whether you want a "Just listed" ad to start automatically after the listing agreement is signed, a "Just sold" ad to start automatically after a listing is sold, or a sphere of influence (SOI) ad to start automatically after a new agent joins the firm, we need data to power them all.

How have your expectations of your management team changed over the past two years?

We've gone through rapid expansion, as have a lot of companies and brokerages, so we've asked our team to take on more. Because of this, I've asked my team for more transparency and collaboration than ever—it's the best way to help us all stay on task and keep pace with innovation.

It's important to systematize and automate what you can so you aren't rethinking everything each time. Great systems lead to consistent results. I believe it's the leader's job to inspire and support the organization's collective responsibility to create a better future for the company, and I empower everyone on my management team to do their part to impact this future.

How do you keep your team competitive?

Hire brilliant and competitive people that align with our core values. Then give them freedom within the company's strategic framework. Try to expose everyone to our customers and partners so they can hear firsthand the changing needs and changing market. After that, its alignment, alignment, alignment.

With so much disruption in real estate, what's your best advice for managing change?

My advice is to embrace change. I've seen this happen in both of the other industries with which I have been involved—music and printing/packaging. There's always going to be disruption. The challenge is to never let disruption distract you from your core values and your core mission. But it *can* help you envisage a better way to get there.

Disruption always makes me reevaluate what the end state will ultimately be for the transaction being contemplated.

16.

Leadership Lens: If you're not growing, you're dying

Laura Brady

Laura Brady

As the founder and president of international luxury real estate auction firm Concierge Auctions, Laura Brady is responsible for leading the company and its aggressive growth.

In less than ten years, she's driven the firm to nearly two billion dollars in sales and placement on Inc. Magazine's list of the fastest-growing companies in America four years in a row. We recently sat down with Laura to ask her views on the current state of real estate leadership.

As a leader, what keeps you up at night?

My pursuit of continued innovation and staying ahead of the curve is what keeps me up at night. Concierge Auctions has been on a strong growth trajectory for 10 years now, and we're always racing to find and retain the best talent, keep a strong pulse on industry changes and constantly beat our prior records.

My most common nightmare is about losing my teeth, which

signifies that important changes are in the works. Ah … the beauty of entrepreneurship! If you're not growing, you're dying.

If you could change one thing in real estate, what would it be?

The biggest problem I'm committed to solving is the lack of transparency and time certainty in real estate transactions. In nearly every other area of our lives, we're able to transact on our chosen time frame, and the terms are clear. Most other purchases can be made digitally and anonymously, if we so choose, but when it comes to real estate, the typical sale process is confusing and lengthy.

We created the Concierge Auctions marketplace to give listing agents and sellers control of the timeline of sale and instill confidence in buyers. All parties can see every offer, real-time, and trust that the final sale price was fair and market-driven.

How have your expectations of your management team changed over the past two years?

In the past two years, we've nearly doubled our annual revenue, employee count and geographic service area, so our leadership team is consistently being held to higher standards. We've added bench strength from both internal and external hires, which has allowed internal candidates to rise from employees to managers to c-suite where earned.

Our leaders are responsible for knowing and reporting on their growth metrics, for fostering collaboration between their teams and for pursuing an "Always be learning" practice of ongoing education.

How do you keep your team competitive?

The first step is that I'm fiercely competitive myself. One of our core values at Concierge Auctions is to "Make history," and in some way or another, every employee competes every day in our business, whether it's to close a deal, launch a marketing campaign more quickly than the last, or to break our prior highest-priced sales records.

We compete not only for ourselves and our business success, but also to better the world. Through our Key for Key™ program in cooperation with Giveback Homes, for every home we sell, we fully fund a home for a family in need. Launched in April of last year, Key for Key™ drives our team towards a higher and common purpose.

With so much disruption in real estate, what's your best advice for managing change?

My best advice is to embrace it. We're wired to be fearful of the unknown, so my philosophy is to not only be aware of but also knowledgeable about as many topics as I can.

Knowledge is power and instills confidence. On average I spend three to four hours every day reading and listening to books, podcasts and news. I not only focus on real estate but also entrepreneurship, history and other finance, tech and business sectors.

17.

Leadership Lens: Paul Boomsma on zigging when everyone zags

Paul Boomsma

With over 20 years of experience in luxury real estate, Paul Boomsma created the highly successful Luxury Portfolio International division for Leading Real Estate Companies of the World, which he continues to lead as president. He also oversees operations and strategic marketing for Leading Real Estate Companies of the World, serving as COO.

Paul began his career marketing luxury office towers and later joined a top residential firm before becoming national marketing director for a major franchise. We recently had the opportunity to sit down with Paul and ask him his thoughts and opinions on the future of what it means to be a leader in real estate.

As a leader, what keeps you up at night?

Fortunately, I sleep very well—however, on the occasion that I lie awake it's always about people. In our business, people are the heart of everything we do. This is especially true in our organization, which is all about networking, collaborating (which is even one of our internal core values) and successfully working together.

Relationships, trust and respect for one another are our keys to success and are central to effective leadership. In fact, we have a fantastic management training program for sales managers called Maestro and in it we have an entire module dedicated to culture, because we know people don't leave jobs, they leave people.

So when I do lay awake at night, it's often because of my concerns about the human side of our business or, more specifically, how to ensure the human side, open communication and personal connections remain strong. This is even more true in this day and age, when we are all so focused on the urgent, moving quickly and firing off email or texting, simply to keep on top. We forget that our digital world, while efficient, removes so much of the intonation, intent and tone behind what we may mean and can so easily be misconstrued.

I am constantly reminding our people that sometimes we all need to stop, take a breath, have a face-to-face meeting or make a phone call simply to limit miscommunication, and ensure we are all on the same page. The truth is, I like everyone to play nice in the sandbox. It can keep me up at night when that doesn't always happen, especially when it can so often have been avoided simply with thoughtful, effective and, most importantly, personal communication.

If you could change one thing in real estate, what would it be?

I have been in real estate for a long time now, and a big part of what I love about our business is how it represents "the dream." We are making people's dreams come true, and that is an incredibly gratifying experience. And yet, I do wish that everyone involved had more realistic expectations. Who knows this better than a real estate agent?

I have so much admiration and respect for agents because of their tenacity, optimism in the face of daily hurdles, work ethic and, perhaps most importantly, their incredible ability to focus on the reality of a situation and continually work on finding on a solution in a constant quest to make someone's dream a reality.

Today's transactions can be so complicated and riddled with fault-finding because buyers and sellers are so conditioned to expect perfection in every home in our reality-TV, do-it-yourself world. What is the real reality? Homes are not perfect. Much of our aging inventory should be expected to have a dent or ding. These little imperfections are the character of our industry and should be embraced. Unfortunately, so often the opposite happens, and what used to be imperfections or quite simply reality, is now escalated into something that makes both sides of the transaction a challenge.

I know I am not alone in saying that I would love to have more sellers understand what it really takes to get their homes ready to sell—and have more buyers understand that a 25-year-old home is not brand new.

How have your expectations of your management team changed over the past two years?

I've always expected my senior leaders to be outstanding representations of our brands, to embrace our culture and to embody everything we stand for. These past two years have not represented any change in what I expect from them.

I am grateful to have so many people on our team that have been with us for five, 10, 15 and even 20 plus years. As a company, we have transformed over that time, not only in what we offer and the breath of services we provide, but in what we mean to our members and to the consumer.

I am so proud we have so many outstanding leaders who have embraced the challenge of change, the reality of market fluctuations, the intensity of global growth and every other significant organizational change we have taken on. Without a strong leadership bench an organization is lost.

Our team is incredibly passionate about what they do, and I believe that comes across in every interaction they have. They are truly the best of the best. The reality is I expect them to be top notch—and they are.

How do you keep your team competitive?

First and foremost, we focus on what we are doing: building and supporting the very best independent brands in the industry, regardless of the competition. While it is always important to keep your eye on the competition, we are driven by what we want and need, what our members need and how we can communicate that directly to the consumer.

We are not just about "keeping up," "getting ahead" or offering things because that is what everyone else is doing. Our network is a collection of successful independent brokerages that built their businesses by zigging when everyone else zagged. Our brokers have always done what was right for them, their clients and their markets. They've done it their own way. We try to embody that same ethos in all that we do.

With so much disruption in real estate, what's your best advice for managing change?

Don't try to "manage" change—evaluate it and embrace it or, if it's not a fit for you, don't. There is always a good reason for change—the question is: is it good for you?

Not all changes or new models or offerings are the right fit for everyone just because they're the new, hot thing. When it isn't in your best interest, or the right fit for your culture or business model, it's of course healthy to spend time analyzing it to determine if you missed an opportunity that someone else may be capitalizing on. Then, update what you're doing to be competitive, or don't. Everyone doesn't need to play in every particular space.

18.

Real estate leaders: Don't hide in your ivory tower

Gill South

Real estate professionals would like to see more transparency, honesty, vision, credibility, accessibility, energy and inspiration from their leadership, according to an informal poll on the industry Facebook group Inman Coast to Coast.

Old-school, top-down hierarchy; "ivory tower" management; and micromanagement in the office are no longer welcome, said the community of Inman readers.

Katie Clancy, Realtor and owner of William Raveis' The Cape House team in Massachusetts, suggested a model in which advisory boards with all the stakeholders set the leadership direction.

Moreover, leaders who can look ahead and see what's coming down the road will be extremely valuable. "I want leaders who are forward-thinking and willing to embrace change," said Laurie Weston Davis, co-owner of Better Homes and Gardens Lifestyle Property Partners. "Leaders who are focused on the long term. It's not about today—it's about five to 10 to 20 years from now."

Training expert Alyssa Hellman, meanwhile, wanted to see a desire by current management to "create more leaders."

Social media guru Katie Lance added, "I want more leaders who understand that it's less about them and more about other people—and elevating the people around them. People who check their ego at the door are the leaders I want to be around."

In a similar vein, Jeff Lobb would like to see the end of what he calls "hit and runs"—when an executive parachutes in to deliver a message, looks at their watch and hightails it out of there before anyone gets the opportunity to have a proper conversation with them. Speaking to Inman later, Lobb elaborated on this point and said disconnected leaders are not doing the industry any favors: "They don't engage with agents or brokers or anybody of any importance," he said. "They become the invisible ghost. They jet in and jet out, their busy schedules don't give them time to connect as a human, to get to know what some of their people are thinking."

As a result, those who operate at the corporate level start to forget what happens on the ground, and they are therefore uninformed when making key decisions, said Lobb, who noted: "As a leader, I have to know what the clients' challenges are. I can't do that by being invisible."

Tracy Freeman, a broker from Coldwell Banker Real Estate in New Jersey, has been heartened by her management's interest in listening to their agents.

"I personally have been involved in think tank sessions where our 'C-suite' invited me and other active agents to give our perspective on what the day-to-day needs of an agent are and how the brand can support those need," Freeman commented on Coast to Coast. Her leaders are therefore able to help address agents' pain points, Freeman told Inman later.

Freeman's regional executive vice president with NRT's Eastern region, Kate Rossi, has organized a listing workshop for agents who are finding the low inventory market challenging. "It's fantastic. It's a pain point, the lack of inventory —it's great to have a leader who can think about this and help at a high level," said Freeman.

Lobb also thinks that top managers should be far more active on social media to give their people some idea of their personality and share insights on how they like to spend their time.

Many top leaders are not active on social media, Lobb said. "They don't want to be known in a world of trust and connecting with people and choose not to share. They have to show they are human," he added. Lobb said Better Homes and Gardens president Sherry Chris exemplifies how to be accessible. "She shows up at events, at parties. She'll post on social on the weekend and she's engaging, she gets it," Lobb told Inman.

Michael Fischer, Coldwell Banker's COO is another leader who is known to post about his hobbies online, making sure he connects with agents at events, Lobb said. Meanwhile, Lobb would like to see better pathways for real estate professionals to move up the ladder in their firms in a transparent way.

When managers are brought in from other industries at the top level, that can be deflating for those toiling away in the company, he said. "I think what frustrates people is the good old boys club," he said.

19.

What quality leadership in a brokerage looks like

Cara Ameer

Imagine a real estate brokerage in which the management's focus is truly 100 percent on agents. Where real estate agents are the customers.

Instead of focusing on the next recruit, sales meeting or metric, the brokerage's management takes the time to pay attention to what's in the house versus what's outside of it. Agents are more than just a number with a sales volume attached to their name.

Which raises the question: Do brokerages really know the agents who choose to hang their license with them? Notice I said choose.

Where agents decide to place their license is a *choice*, and agents have many companies to choose from. When agents hang their license, they are choosing to not only make money for themselves but also for the brokerage that they are affiliating with.

Although obvious, it's easy to forget: agents are the lifeblood of any brokerage, and without them, the brokerage ceases to exist.

Below is my opinion of what leadership at a brokerage level would look like in an ideal world—in all the facets of a real estate agent's career.

Learning the business

Recognizing the importance of agents, managers would truly serve as mentors and coaches or put people in place to meet this need.

Serving as a mentor or coach means much more than just a passing "How's it going?," "Congratulations on your latest listing, sale or closing" or "Is there anything I can do for you?" Higher-ups would take time to really study and understand your business.

Just because they can generate a report showing the agents' production for their entire career from the MLS with the press of a button, does not mean they really understand.

A real leader would help agents deconstruct their businesses and analyze every aspect from all angles.

- How is the agent getting his or her business?
- Where is it coming from?
- Where do they want to go with it?
- What kind of roadmap can the broker help them map out to get there?
- What are their pain points and weaknesses?
- What is holding them back from getting to the next level?

And management would consider asking this question: How is the brokerage hampering or hindering their success?

Management that fears and/or loathes hearing the truth need not be in a leadership capacity. Surface-level suggestions and pseudo-solutions need not apply.

Mentoring or coaching

In a perfect world, the manager or designated "mentor/coach" would meet regularly with agents one-on-one to serve as an accountability coach and sounding board.

There would be coaching programs tailored to agents at a variety of levels in the brokerage from brand new agents, lower to mid-level producing agents and top producers because needs and challenges vary greatly from group to group.

Keeping in touch with the basics

Whether an agent had his or her very first listing presentation or was competing for a tough listing and needed to pull out all the stops, the broker would do something unheard of—actually go on the listing appointment with them.

When was the last time your management went back into the field to make a listing presentation, show a home or handle a negotiation?

Reconnecting with these basic tasks would keep leaders close to the very process they are supposed to support. The broker would have a strategy session with the agent in advance of the meeting that would go beyond the typical "armchair advice."

Marketing support would be provided in advance, much like an ad agency that was preparing for that big "pitch," with the goal of giving the agent the support he or she needed when walking in the sellers' door.

Planning for productivity

Meetings would be thoughtful, well-planned events. They would not be held "just because" and filled with dog-and-pony show vendors to have their 10-minute "spiel" in front of agents.

Any vendors that would be invited into the brokerage's tribe would be vetted, respected and have core values on par with that of the brokerage's.

Leadership would dig deeper before letting just any service provider or vendor have face time with the intent of soliciting business from their agents.

By this, I mean no builders who don't play nice in the sandbox with agents all of the time, forget fly-by-night inspectors who are new on the scene and never again another mortgage company that brings a box of donuts no one really wants to eat anyway.

Besides, referrals are not a one-way street. Why should these vendors—who have not necessarily earned the right to a referral—have an at-bat in front of a large agent audience when the brokerage's agents will likely never receive customer referrals from these same people?

Real leaders are respectful of their agents' time and information needs, and recognize that an hour is better spent on relevant issues, training and topics of discussion without vendors pitches.

Being accountable

Ownership and management would be 100 percent accountable to their agents. They would actually understand, have tested and know every product, program and offering within their company, whether an independent brokerage or part of a national firm.

Any questions about the brokerage's services from agents would be answered in a quick and practical manner versus kicking the agent down the road to another department.

Exemplary leadership would encourage and initiate open dialogue and hold "town hall" style meetings to engage in constructive discussion and debate and to be better aware of concerns, challenges and broken processes or systems that need addressing.

Agents could share their thoughts and proposed solutions. Management would be frank about what could be changed and the reasons behind the decision making rather than dodging the same concerns year after year.

True leaders would actively track said issues so that they don't get brushed over or forgotten. They'd have a goal of resolving as many as they could to prevent the same conversations about unaddressed issues again and again.

They would keep agents informed of the status of these matters without agents having to ask.

Adding value

Brokerages would see where they could add value to their agents and not nickel-and-dime them for every little thing. It's the little things, not the big things, that tend to build up over time and cause agents to rethink their arrangement.

Agents are charged enough in the real estate business as it is. Real leaders take time to understand agent frustration points and proactively manage them rather than react after the fact. Trying to rationalize the "grass isn't always greener" response along with a shoulder shrug each time a productive agent leaves for another brokerage is not getting to the root of the problem.

Recruiting

Speaking of agents, recruiting would shift from a "somebody, anybody, everybody who ever expressed interest in working in real estate" mentality to a quality approach.

Thoughtful consideration would be given to determine if the current company infrastructure could truly support the workload required when onboarding new recruits, whether a newbie or seasoned veteran.

Commitments made would be commitments honored, but not at the expense or detriment of existing agents in the company. Side arrangements and special treatment would not be for a special few.

An in-depth evaluation of a potential new hire would be undertaken, much like a job interview with closer examination of the agent's work history, track record and professional reputation whether that was in real estate or another profession.

Evolving

Leaders would stay on the cutting edge of industry issues and what's next to ensure their agents had the tools to stay ahead of the curve, not catch up to it after the fact. They would serve as thought leaders, industry challengers and disruptors, encouraging their agents to do the same.

Proactive leadership fosters stability and sustainability among management with special focus on the brokers that have front-line responsibility for managing offices, something that is tough to do in the "bottom line" environment that is prevalent in the real estate industry.

Dynamic leaders would devise a compensation model to keep good managers who are empowered to lead versus babysit offices whereby managing agents is akin to herding cats.

Being transparent

Exemplary leadership fosters transparency. Leaders would conduct an annual "state of the brokerage" for their agents that went beyond the total sales volume and number of transactions for the prior year as typical sales rallies depict.

Also explained would be the actual costs that were incurred with running the brokerage for the past year and what the projected costs would be for the current year.

The debt, expenses and the financial investment needed for new projects and priorities would be discussed. In addition, any financial incentives and profit realized as a result of joint ventures or "affiliated arrangements" from preferred mortgage, title and home warranty providers would be disclosed.

If agents are encouraged to support company affiliated service providers, they have a right to know what's in it for the brokerage.

Although old-school thinking may fear sharing this information, emotionally intelligent leaders say the more that agents are "in the know," the more they are likely to understand the big picture. It's easy to complain when you only know part of the story.

If all of this sounds like some lofty, idyllic Neverland proposition, think again.

With barriers to entry into the profession extremely low, high turnover and a generally small pond of recruits, both experienced and brand new, to fish from, the real estate industry is ripe for renovation.

To raise the bar, we must redefine and revolutionize leadership in real estate. The industry is already changing before our eyes. Isn't it time for all of us to become agents of change?

20.

7 things real estate leaders should never do

Spyro Kemble

Problems arise in real estate all the time. Just the other day, I found myself in the middle of a complex and convoluted transaction. Like any smart real estate agent, I sought the opinion of my brokers.

As I sat across the desk from their wealth of knowledge, I quickly remembered the importance of great leadership. After 10 minutes under their sound counsel, I had a fresh perspective and solution to my problem.

This desk-side encounter got me thinking about the importance of leadership in our industry. Though many would say that the days of traditional brokerages are quickly fading, I happen to disagree.

I still believe there is a place and a need for the traditional brokerage firm in our industry, one that leads by mentorship and by example.

The three-fold question then becomes:

> 1. What does great leadership look like?
>
> 2. What does it not look like?
>
> 3. Is there room at the table to sit on both sides of the desk?

Before I continue, I want to let you know that the firm I chose to hang my broker's license under now is only my second brokerage in my 30-plus years in the industry. Obviously, I don't make a habit of playing musical chairs with my brokerage.

And between my tenure in real estate and my time spent serving as the president of my association, I know the difference between good and bad leadership.

What great leadership looks like

Having had the privilege of working under great leadership for the past 11 years, here are the do's of great leadership as I see them.
 Great leadership:

- Provides accessibility to the entire team
- Creates a cooperative culture among its agents with information flowing freely, working as a team and not as individuals
- Offers layers of support in all aspects of business including weekly workshops, meetings and training on new technology
- Operates with total transparency and makes the compensation structure known to all with no secret dealings
- Shows 100 percent dedication to its agents and their quest for market share and long-term success
- Evolves constantly in regards to image, brand, resources, training programs and technology
- Honors fiduciary duties to its agents by never forgetting that agents are the cornerstones of the company

7 don'ts of real estate leadership

Perhaps more critical, there's a list of don'ts that I've seen in my career. Great leadership does not do the following:

1. Compete with its agents

Meaning, to be an effective leader or manager, you cannot be in direct or indirect competition with your agents to list or sell. In most areas, the ratio of clients-to-agents is such that many agents are competing for business from the same small client pool. You cannot sit on both seats and expect to have your agent's best interest at heart.

2. Divide its attention

As a leader, your focus must be your agents. Being both a manager and an agent is like being a cop and a firefighter at the same time. Both are full-time jobs.

Think about this logically. If a manager is showing listings, taking buyers out to see property, holding broker previews and open houses, navigating escrows and interfacing with his or her own clients, how much time is left to provide support to agents?

And where is the manager's attention being focused? On you and your clients, or on his or her own business and clients?

At best, a manager, who also operates as an agent, has a divided interest. At minimum, he or she will have limited time for his or her fellow agents, and he or she will end-up competing against fellow agents for potential clients. This is far from a win-win.

3. Offer secret deals as a recruiting or retention method

One of the biggest mistakes a firm can make is a lack of transparency. Too often, I have seen companies offer secret deals as an incentive to retain or attract agents to join the brokerage.

Newsflash: These deals never stay secret, and sooner rather than later, other agents find out that they are not that special anymore and some new hotshot got a better deal. When these secret deals are discovered it causes dissension in the company. Plus, it's a non-sustainable formula.

I'm reminded of a friend who planned to join our brokerage long before he actually did. Every time he talked about leaving his brokerage, his company kept throwing money at him to stay.

The gimmick worked for a while, but as the company did not

have the support, culture and many other factors it needed to grow his business, the agent eventually left.

Please don't misunderstand, I totally endorse different levels of compensation and splits based on performance, as long it is consistent and transparent to all.

4. Create a business model with the emphasis on selling the company

It used to be that selling a successful brokerage was a by-product of having built a successful company with substantial market share.

These days, brokerages launch with the goal of building a company that can be sold to a national chain within five or 10 years.

5. Make technology its cornerstone

AI and technology are very important components in a growing and successful brokerage, but they are secondary to hands-on management and daily human interaction.

6. Foster an attitude of individuals or lone rangers

You will never realize your potential or find success if you are working as an individual where the flow of information is not part of your daily routine.

If there is a disconnect between you and your brokerage, there will be an inherent disconnect between you and your clients.

7. Dishonor its fiduciary duties to its agents

Personally, I would like to be the boss of everything. However, as professionals, we have a fiduciary duty when it comes to the roles we play.

What I'm saying is that the ethical decision between "can" we sit in both seats or "should" we sit in both seats, needs to be addressed.

I am reminded of a quote from the movie *Jurassic Park* that said: "Your scientists were so preoccupied with whether they could, they didn't stop to think if they should."

That same question is what I am posing to our industry: just because we can, should we?

At the end of the day, a true leader knows which chair he or she should sit in.

21.

What's the no. 1 thing you'd change about the real estate industry?

Gill South

If the real estate community had a magic wand that could change one thing about the real estate industry, improving industry leadership would be at the top of the wish list for many, as would raising the barriers to entry to becoming an agent in the field, increased transparency, and better benefit offerings from brokerages, according to a conversation that unfolded on the Inman Coast to Coast Facebook group.

As Michelle Poccia, associate broker at Keller Williams Capital District put it: "(It is) an industry so full of titles, yet so (de)void of the kind of leadership it needs."

National, state and local associations are often a "hot mess of (un)business like practices," with too many separate entities creating an environment of slow change, she said. Brokerages were operated or influenced by the "volunteer leadership flavor of the year."

Worthington, Ohio-based Keller Williams Capital Partners' Jodi Beekman, a member of her branch's agent leadership council, told Inman that creating strong leadership from top to bottom at a real estate company is a challenge. Beekman appreciates the proactive leadership from Keller Williams' co-founder Gary Keller, but with independent contractors and a sprawling franchise network, it is hard to maintain these standards throughout the company, she said. "The independent contractors say, 'I can do whatever I like,' so it's like herding cats," she added.

In the Coast to Coast exchange, Beekman disagreed with a number of calls for higher barriers to entry in the industry. "A higher barrier to entry only makes it more difficult for the next generation of agents. What do we do about the ones already licensed that are wreaking havoc today?" she asked in the comments.

Talking to Inman later, she said: "I don't think the problem is in the brand new people. It's the people who have been doing it forever who don't want to accept that their way could be done better."

Meanwhile for Lisa Sevajian, an independent brokerage co-owner of Bentley's in Andover, Massachusetts, her wish would be to see brokerages offering retirement plans, insurance plans, disability plans and childcare options, for starters.

"Agents work for years and years helping our clients make smart choices, yet we rarely do so ourselves when it comes to building lifelong income, family wealth, investment opportunities," she commented on Coast to Coast.

Sevajian and her business partners are providing their 34 agents with leads for free and bringing in experts to help them make savvy investment and personal finance decisions.

Talking to Inman, Sevajian, who worked at Coldwell Banker and Re/Max before coming to Bentley's, said she was raised by her grandmother, a broker and agent who was selling well into her 80s because she couldn't financially afford to retire, even though she was one of the highest producers in the market.

The broker-owner wants her agents to be earning good six-figure salaries so they can build "legacy careers," she said. And to be clever with their commission checks.

But maybe "what does the industry want?" is the wrong question, said Mary McKane, managing broker of Levi Rodgers Real Estate Group at Re/Max Military City, in San Antonio, Texas. Surely the more pertinent question is, "what would the consumer like to see if they had a magic wand?" she suggested in Coast to Coast.

Speaking to Inman later, she said it was easy for those in the real estate industry to get "tunnel vision."

Consumers have more information in their hands than ever before, and often they become overwhelmed.

"They need someone to guide them with the process, and collectively we don't do a very good job of that. We protect information, worried about where it goes, yet we are a customer service industry, this is their biggest investment and the process needs to be very transparent," she said.

The system would work a lot better if people collaborated and helped everybody rather than "hoarding information," she said.

22.

7 ways real estate leaders can improve their social media

Marian McPherson

Social media, in many ways, has made the world a smaller place. People who once seemed out of reach, such as celebrities, politicians and leaders, now pop up in our feeds every day, posting pictures and videos of their personal lives and even engaging in conversation with the people they serve and entertain.

BGHRE CEO Sherry Chris

According to a recent thread in Facebook group Inman Coast to Coast, many real estate leaders are struggling to follow suit and embrace the unique opportunity social media platforms provide—the ability to step out of the "ivory tower" and connect with their brokers and agents on a deeper, more authentic and human level.

Here's what four social media dynamos—Better Homes and Gardens Real Estate CEO Sherry Chris, Real Estate Webmasters founder and CEO Morgan Carey, Douglas Elliman Western Region president Sharran Srivatsaa and Zillow CEO Spencer Rascoff—and a few other social media experts have to say about making meaningful connections online.

Don't force it

Although social media yields positive personal and business results, and has become an integral part of the real estate industry, each expert agreed that "forcing" your way into social media is a surefire way to fail.

Chris and Carey said social media is simply an extension of their personalities and dedication to connecting with their brokers, agents, consumers and wider network.

"You have to want to do it. You can't suddenly turn 'social' on," said Chris. "Doing it halfheartedly is not what I recommend at all."

Chris says she's always put an emphasis on adding a personal touch, which includes mailing handwritten cards, visiting broker offices and attending special events. For her, social media has only served as a tool to make those things easier.

"It's an all-encompassing communication and caring that leads me to be a strong contributor on social," she said.

Carey echoed Chris' sentiments, noting that he's always been comfortable building relationships online since people in his generation grew up with the internet.

"We grew up talking on bulletin boards, on bb [blackberry] boards, b-bulletin boards [a dial-up messaging system], and chats," he said. "So I think for someone from my generation (I'm 38), it's a lot more organic for us versus some of the leaders who didn't necessarily grow up with the internet in the same way."

Carey says a leader's choice to engage on social media is ultimately a personal one, and it depends on that person's natural inclination to share or not to share.

On the management side, Coldwell Banker director of media engagement Lindsay Listanski noted the importance of keeping social media optional—social media and marketing directors should never pressure their execs into being active on social, especially if participation could become a burden or distraction from other tasks.

"Not every leader needs to have a huge social media presence," she said. "If it doesn't come natural to you, figure out a couple areas where you can add value."

Understand how to use each platform

Facebook. Twitter. Instagram. Snapchat. Each platform has its own rules, strengths and weaknesses—something that can befuddle the social media newbie. Listanski said every exec should have a clear understanding of every platform they'd like to join as well as a solid posting strategy.

"No copy and pasting across the board," she said.

Chris's social media strategy is the perfect example of one that has been thought out and well-planned. Here's how she breaks it down:

- LinkedIn is all about business. She reposts interesting business articles and blogs and comments on colleagues' statuses.

- Twitter is a mix of business and personal. Chris said she'll tweet about BHGRE and her personal hobbies, such as interior design, fashion and the arts.

- She maintains two Facebook profiles. On her business profile, she shares business articles, the accomplishments of her network and business ideas. On her personal page, she shares business news but mainly focuses on her family and friends.

- Chris says Instagram is all about sharing people and places, and it lends itself to a little more edginess. "If someone wants to know more about me, then Instagram is the place to go," she said.

Once you understand how a platform works, you'll be able to understand which ones fit you and which ones can be left behind.

Rascoff says Snapchat "didn't stick" for him, but he's been able to effectively use Facebook, Twitter and LinkedIn to connect with his network.

"I've always used Twitter, and I naturally gravitate to it because I like the brevity of it," he said. "Over time I've added Facebook and Instagram, and I write longer articles on LinkedIn."

> Thanks to my 12 year old daughter for teaching me iphone trick: swipe left-to-right on the bottom of iphone screen to move from app-to-app.
> — Spencer Rascoff (@spencerrascoff) February 13, 2018

Be authentic

Social media has given real estate leaders a unique platform to connect with their networks in a direct and honest way. While some stick to "vanilla" posts (canned responses to simple issues and prepared advertising content) others dive right in—sharing what they care about, who they care about and engaging in thought-provoking conversations.

Zillow CEO Spencer Rascoff says authenticity is about understanding when you have something meaningful to add to the conversation. "Don't weigh in on topics if you don't have something to say," said Rascoff in an emailed statement to Inman.

Sharran Srivatsaa

Douglas Elliman Western Region president Sharran Srivatsaa says he's able to maintain his authenticity on social media by maintaining full control of what he posts.

"Very simple. Don't farm out your social media," he said. "That takes away from the authenticity of the leader not just for that post but for anything that leader ever wants to say on his or her platform in the future. Leaders have a responsibility to engage with their tribes personally on social media and it is disrespectful to their audience when they farm out all their social media for someone else to manage."

For those who need some extra encouragement to move beyond "vanilla" posts, social media coach Katie Lance says hopping on Instagram stories or Snapchat to share behind-the-scenes photos and videos of your day is a good first step.

The stories are quick to produce, they disappear after 24 hours and they allow your brokers, agents and network to have a better understanding of who you are and what you do.

Mix business and pleasure

Listanski says the most influential real estate leaders on social media maintain a "yin and yang" balance on their pages—a mix of the rational (business) and emotional (personal).

Carey relishes the ability to share his personal life with his network and said he thinks of his Facebook profile as a gratitude journal.

"I post a lot about my wife, my kids, my dogs, my farm, the things that really make me happy," he said.

Morgan Carey

For Carey, sharing those positive moments allows his network to have a better understanding of what motivates him and what matters to him outside of real estate. Furthermore, he said sharing your humanity helps build trust—an integral part of making sure you have a team and network that will be there for the long haul.

On the other hand, Rascoff says he doesn't share a lot about his family life, but he will occasionally share a cute picture

of his dogs or his kids—just a little something that allows his followers to get a sense of who he is outside of Zillow.

Decide how you'll deal with criticism

Figuring out how to deal with criticism is a pain point for many
leaders on social media, and each exec has a different way of handling it.

"Run toward problems," said Carey of his approach to online
criticism. "You have the opportunity to showcase how you conduct
yourself in the face of adversity in that scenario."

Carey said he'll engage in conversation with an open mindset
and, often times, the result is him gaining a new friend or learning
a new way to improve his business. In other instances, he chooses
to shut down the conversation when it becomes clear that someone
wants to argue for the sake of arguing.

Chris says she prefers to handle criticisms offline. She has a
team who keeps an eye on BHGRE's various social media pages,
and they acknowledge any criticisms, questions or concerns. From
there, they'll get the commenter's personal information so they can
reach out to address the problem one-on-one.

Rascoff, who has seen and heard his fair share of fiery comments while at Zillow, says "although there is much to be learned
from those who disagree with you, I try to ignore the haters and
trolls."

Stay aware of your role as a brand ambassador and leader

While the key to being successful on social media requires authenticity and a willingness to step into the fray, it's important for execs
to remember they're the face of a brand, and anything they say can
reflect on the company as a whole.

Spencer Rascoff

Rascoff says a few tweets he made "about the importance of having a long-term orientation when running a company" on the eve of an earnings call caused an internal company dilemma—his public relations team thought followers could interpret the tweets "as us being likely to have bad upcoming earnings results."

Rascoff and his team eventually decided to keep the tweets since deleting them could cause more speculation. What did he learn?

"Public company executives have to be extra careful about what they post, and when," he said.

Beyond maintaining a positive personal and brand image, brokerage industry expert Russ Cofano says execs must be thoughtful about what they post because it could pose legal issues.

"The first question that should always be asked is whose 'voice' is the person posting on social media representing. For CEOs, it is very difficult to do so other than as the leader of a company," said Cofano.

"If the 'posting voice' is on behalf of the company or could be construed that way, there are plenty of business/political issues that can come into play, but the primary legal issues revolve around defamation, the release of confidential information into the public domain and in real estate, comments that might be construed as anti-competitive and possibly anti-trust violations."

Cofano says execs would be wise to have their PR teams look over any social media statements to make sure they're not inadvertently releasing nonpublic information—something he says could impact a public company's stock price and create securities laws violations.

"If done right, social media can be a powerful tool that many executives use for the benefit of their organization," he said. "At the same time, executives should understand all of the negative business, political and legal issues that may arise from a misguided post."

Bring the online, offline

While social media is great for sparking a friendship or partnership, those relationships can't thrive without in-person interactions.

Spark Tank Media CEO Jeff Lobb says execs need to stop jetting in and out of conferences and other events without talking to the brokers and agents who help their company succeed.

"Don't be above the celebration, be a part of it," Lobb said. "We sometimes forget these are the people who make the company work. So, we should never be above anybody."

Lobb says execs should prepare to be put on the spot or asked questions they don't have answers to. But those potentially nerve-wracking moments shouldn't stop them from interacting with their network. In fact, Lobb says allowing your team to see you in those situations makes you more human.

"Fortunately, those who share and engage and make themselves more human gain the trust and the visibility of others, especially when it comes to the recruiting phase or the franchise sale," he said.

Each of the execs said they've been able to use their social media experiences to "minimize the distance" between themselves and their brokers, agents and consumers.

"I try to bring up things I've learned about people's recent activities through their social posts when I meet them because it minimizes the distance from when we last caught up," said Rascoff. "If I'm meeting with an agent I know well, I'll check their Facebook or Twitter to see if anything notable happened in their lives—like a new team member starting or taking a great vacation—and ask about that."

"I think early on with social media that would have been kind of odd, but it's such a common practice now," he added. "Social media is like homework for live conversations."

23.

Leadership Lens: The one thing that doesn't change is change

Sarita Dua

Sarita Dua is the principal broker and MAPS Mastery Coach at Keller Williams Realty Professionals in Portland, Oregon. Founded in 1983, Keller Williams Realty Inc. is an international real estate company with over 930 offices located across the world. The company began franchising in 1991, and following years of phenomenal growth and success, the company recently claimed it had become no. 1 in units and sales volume in 2017.

The company has succeeded by treating its associates as partners, and it shares its knowledge, policy control and company profits on a system-wide basis.

We recently had the opportunity to sit down with Sarita and pick her brain on what the future of real estate leadership holds for 2018.

As a leader, what keeps you up at night?

How to add value to my people. How to create a culture that is more than results and numbers—to be at a place they want to be where their opinions are valued and they are excited about working with our clients and prospects.

If you could change one thing in real estate, what would it be?

Facebook! Seriously too many agents online and not enough of them out there in the field working, learning and growing. The brokerage infighting and the subtle and not so subtle direct jabs. I am excited about agents from every brokerage and every walk of life. Everyone has a choice. But to say there is only one option and one is better than the other is short-sighted and not the way to make this industry better.

How have your expectations of your management team changed over the past two years?

They really haven't. It is always relationships first. I guess the only element from a digital world is the expectation that we are always available and we have to be even more responsive. We have stepped up to that challenge. At the end of the day, clients will need us when they need us, and we want to be there and available to answer questions.

How do you keep your team competitive?

Training on systems and processes. Sharing wins and losses and lessons learned. In depth market knowledge and overview. Encouraging reading, doing book clubs, sharing articles and videos.

I care for them and want everyone to grow individually (and personally) so they can be their very best self.

With so much disruption in real estate, what's your best advice for managing change?

The only thing that doesn't change is change itself.

While it is good to know what direction we are headed in, you can't get paralyzed due to impending change, nor can you change what you do today for a future problem or issue.

I believe this business is all about relationships, and as long as we have that and hold it near and dear to our hearts, we are ready for any change that comes our way.

24.

Leadership Lens: Is the appetite for true disruption here?

Zvi Band

Zvi Band is the founder and CEO of Contactually, an intelligent customer relationship management CRM platform for real estate brokers and agents. Zvi founded Contactually back in 2011. An engineer and a CEO, he also actively fosters a strong DC Tech Community and created Proudly Made in DC to continue the support of the greater community. Tony Cappaert co-founded Contactually and now leads up all customer-facing efforts as COO. He's an ex-Microsoft project manager, an MIT alum, karaoke star and lover of all things outdoors and fermented.

We recently got the opportunity to sit down with Zvi and pick his brain about where real estate leadership is headed in 2018.

As a leader, what keeps you up at night?

Maintaining the right balance between innovation and consistency. It's a sliding scale, and we've never been quite comfortable at any point in the spectrum.

We've had times where we've embraced too much of the "move fast and break things" mindset, which introduced a lot of innovation to the industry, yet too much regression for something brokers and agents rely on. The pendulum has swung in the opposite direction, where we were so focused on shoring up what we had that we remained stagnant and started to lose our sheen relative to industry expectations.

Knowing that we provide a mission-critical platform that needs to constantly change—we've gained comfort in knowing that we'll never be comfortable, and a healthy level of tension and stress is what's needed to maintain that right balance.

If you could change one thing in real estate, what would it be?

I rewrote my answer to this prompt a few times before doing a root cause analysis on the underlying issue. And it's, to no surprise, the institutional resistance to change.

I'm thankful that there are enough voices talking about the need for change, however I question if some of the conversations—and fear—are going deep enough. The fear we see being cast from the stage is still an indicator that maybe the appetite for true disruption isn't there yet.

Will there be a time where the right people get around a blank piece of paper, draw out how the industry could operate today, and make it happen? We'd be in a very different world.

How have your expectations of your management team changed over the past two years?

I'm thankful enough to have seen the company—and our team—increase in size. Stanford professors Robert I. Sutton and Huggy Rao framed a core leadership challenge of a scaling company as a decision of embracing a Catholic or Buddhist strategy. Does one try and enforce consistency in how each team operates, or do you let each team adapt to the realities of how they need to work?

As we've grown, we've become more reliant on strong people managers who can take the overarching goals for the company, and translate that into how each member of their team can contribute to that while doing their best work.

How do you keep your team competitive?

By embracing change in the culture ourselves. We can skip over the "hire great people part"—of course we try our best to build a diverse and excellent internal talent pool.

Beyond that, we've coded into our core values not only the things we expect to remain consistent, but an underlying desire for change and innovation. Building off that, we have a plethora of arrows in our quiver—"Leadership School" to improve our managers, an annual professional development fund for every employee, internal innovation days, brown bags and external speakers.

But the hardest thing we've had to gain comfort with is having to part ways with people we love because they or their role no longer represents where you want to go.

With so much disruption in real estate, what's your best advice for managing change?

To channel Jeff Bezos from 20+ years ago—what won't change? That's the question we all too often skip over, however, embracing disruption relies on having a strong grasp of the constants.

Residential property is still the largest asset class in the world, and for the vast majority of consumers, their most expensive purchase. The complexity of the transaction, the ever-changing market dynamics, the emotional and picky nature of consumers and the fact that no two properties are alike all lend themselves to the high likelihood that a human navigator still has high utility.

Layered on top of that are the values that one believes your team cannot deviate from, and serve as the foundation of your culture. The culture will shift, and the values themselves may move as well, but establishing that every employee has a common underlying operating system further creates that foundation. The wording might alter year over year, but we've always championed being user-first and transparent, with a strong belief in innovation and ownership.

With those locked in, set the expectation that everything else has to change.

25.

Leadership Lens: Charlie Young on playing offense

Charlie Young

Charlie Young

Coldwell Banker CEO Charlie Young first joined the Coldwell Banker brand in 2004 after an extensive career in business management, field operations, marketing and real estate operations. Initially, he served as senior vice president of marketing and later was promoted to chief operating officer.

Young spearheaded several innovative programs during his first five years with Coldwell Banker as it became the first national brand in the real estate industry to use video in marketing efforts, develop a Facebook app and a standalone luxury home website. He also guided the brand's 100th anniversary celebration in 2006.

We recently got the opportunity to sit down with Charlie and pick his brain about where real estate leadership is headed in 2018.

As a leader, what keeps you up at night?

Overall, I think Coldwell Banker is well positioned to tackle future challenges. We have the right mindset and we have leverage that others don't have—a great brand, unrivaled network and access to more data than anyone.

What keeps me up at night is execution. Are we properly leveraging all our resources and tools? Are we focusing on the right disrupters and ignoring distractions? At the brand level and the Realogy level, we need to put the agent first when thinking about these questions, while not losing sight of the consumer.

We need to position and empower our agents to meet the changing expectations of today's consumer. A consumer that has come to expect instant, seamless, on-demand information and service from the likes of Uber, Amazon and Airbnb.

If you could change one thing in real estate, what would it be?

The question I hear again and again is: "How is the real estate industry going to leverage big data?" At Coldwell Banker our belief is that big data is essential to empowering our agents. That's why we created CBx close to five years ago.

I'd like to see the real estate industry as a whole leverage data streams more effectively—we need to make our data more accessible and usable, and we need to pay attention to the right outside data to benefit the whole real estate transaction.

In thinking about how we can use data to improve the whole real estate transaction we also need to push ourselves as an industry to become more user friendly. As an example, we need to shorten the amount of time from offer to close. Data and technology are critical to getting us there.

How have your expectations of your management team changed over the past two years?

My expectations for my management team both in Madison and the management teams of Coldwell Banker brokerages across the country haven't changed dramatically over the past two years. I've always expected the best from myself and those around me. And as

I've seen my team and Coldwell Banker offices across the country deliver again and again, my expectations continue to rise.

In addition, as a brand, we've focused on coaching and mentorship, which is occurring at the broker-owner and manager level across the country.

How do you keep your team competitive?

By focusing on big goals and holding ourselves to the highest standard both professionally and as people. We must also stay attuned to what our agents are hearing and seeing on the ground.

With so much disruption in real estate, what's your best advice for managing change?

Play offense, not defense. We're in the midst of epic change now—we're beyond disruption. It's happening. And I think it's one of the most exciting times to be in real estate. So as for managing change, I say embrace it. Identify your strengths and leverage them in everything you do.

We focus on the size and scope of our network. Gen Blue has the highest quality agents in the best markets. We tout the value of our brand—a brand marked by all the right things: a focus on high-quality experiences, innovation, trust and integrity.

When we look at disrupters and new entrants, we consider the insight or outside perspective they've brought to our industry and then we think, *how can we make this work at scale?* What does our history, in terms of breadth and depth of data, and our years of qualitative experience teach us about how to integrate new tools or processes? Put simply, we want to focus on the data-driven insights, products and services that will empower agents to succeed.

26.

What real estate leadership needs to succeed

Bernice Ross

Whether you're a brokerage, an agent-led team or an individual agent, you probably have never given any thought to two key, but virtually invisible, components of leadership—what is required to create a space where success can occur and the "glue" that it takes to hold it all together.

As real estate's thought leaders prepare to meet in Palm Springs for Disconnect in the Desert, Brad Inman has been "obsessing over leadership in real estate." Those of us attending Disconnect have received links to articles such as Amazon's 14 Leadership Principles as well as the military's "11 Leadership Principles" that dates back to 1948.

Inman has also surveyed its readers to discover what they expect from their leaders, while contributors have been penning posts with their takes on leadership.

What virtually all books, articles and seminars on leadership address is the "how to," and the "who you need to be." There is no discussion, however, about a third component that is vital to leadership: creating the "space" where leadership can occur in the first place.

The 'space' at Disconnect

At Disconnect in the Desert, Brad Inman is creating the space where the industry's thought leaders will gather to ultimately create "The Real Estate Leadership Manifesto." But what goes into that process?

Inman staff will spend tremendous amounts of time coordinating the hundreds of details that are required to conduct a successful conference.

This includes identifying, vetting and prepping moderators and speakers; all the details about the stage, video and AV; badges, food and drinks for events; and this year, nature hikes, horseback riding or visiting a museum to break away from the traditional "space" where real estate conferences generally occur.

In this case, the staff and the moderators, are holding the space for the conversation, connection and networking to occur.

Creating the agent team 'space'

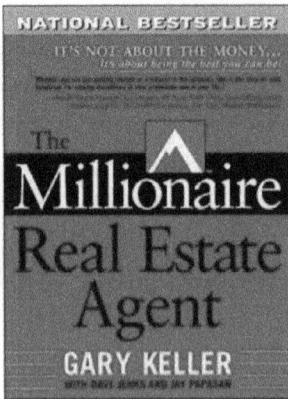

Gary Keller's The Millionaire Real Estate Agent

To illustrate a slightly different notion of "space," consider how the team model of real estate evolved beginning with Gary Keller's *The Millionaire Real Estate Agent.*

The book outlined the steps required to become a "seventh-level business owner" by developing an agent team.

Keller Williams then created an environment (space) that was user-friendly to teams, had specific systems to follow in creating a team, trained its agents on those tools and systems, and encouraged agents to co-brand their team on equal footing with the Keller Williams brand. In other words, it created a space where teams could thrive.

By the same token, the brokerage creates a space, a container if you will, that also enables its agents to conduct transactions.

This includes staff, maintenance of the physical office, the regulatory requirements the brokerage must follow, the technology systems, the company website, plus whatever other services the brokerage provides.

Without the brokerage, agents lacking a broker's license would be unable to conduct transactions.

Creating brokerage culture

When it comes to brokerage leadership, culture is key. But how does a broker create culture?

One critical component is how the leader sets up the space: Is it collaborative or competitive? Revenue focused or customer focused? Does it have a flat or a hierarchal organization, etc.?

Other aspects include the types of people the leader hires to fill that space as well as the policies, procedures and systems that allow the brokerage and the people within the space to function in it.

Leaders need space *and* 'glue'

Although the "space" issues are visible, the "glue," (what holds everything together), is invisible and normally goes unnoticed until something goes wrong.

For example, agents are often the glue that keeps feuding buyers and sellers in the deal when both parties are demanding to cancel.

In terms of brokerage leadership, the unsung heroes and heroines are often the leader's "right-hand" person whose responsibility is to keep everything together and running smoothly.

They organize the leader's life, serve as gatekeepers, free the leader up from the details that would pull them off focus and help the leader stay on track when they're in danger of running off the rails.

Other parts of the "glue" include the staff member who can always be counted on to go the extra mile when an agent needs a quick turnaround on a project, the agents who support each other by providing opinions of value or the person who always bakes a cake for the monthly office birthday party.

This "glue" leads to trust and can even result in what many brokers and agents call "their business family."

As I noted in my column several weeks ago, based on over 50 interviews with successful women brokers from across the country, agents want to know that their broker "has their back."

Furthermore, many agents enjoy being part of a business family that works together, plays together and contributes to the community.

Important questions for your business

- What is the nature of the "space" in your brokerage? Is it the right fit for you?

- Who holds space for you so that you can be better in your role, regardless if you are an agent, manager, team lead or broker?

- Which individuals are the "glue" in your business and personal life—the ones you can really count on, no matter what?

When you identify who is holding space for you and providing the glue in your business or personal life, take the time to express your thanks for how those people make your life and your business better.

27.

Leadership Lens: Collaborate, support, mentor and celebrate

Diane Ramirez

Diane Ramirez

Diane M. Ramirez is the chairman and chief executive officer of Halstead Real Estate. Under her leadership, the firm has grown from its original goal of three storefront offices in the most important communities in Manhattan to its current size of nearly three dozen strategically located offices, with 1,300 agents throughout Manhattan, Brooklyn, Queens, Riverdale, the Hamptons, Hudson Valley, New Jersey and Fairfield County, Connecticut.

We recently sat down with Diane to pick her brain about the future of real estate leadership.

As a leader, what keeps you up at night?

I have made a point over my career to be as organized and forward-thinking as possible. At the end of the day, this has generally allowed me to sleep soundly knowing that I have accomplished everything I possibly can and that tomorrow will be the start of new opportunities and challenges.

Halstead has always been known as an innovative firm, and so on the nights that do keep me up, I am thinking about how we can improve the ways we implement our new tools and ideas so we encourage and achieve the adoption we know is possible.

If you could change one thing in real estate, what would it be?

The fact that real estate is commission-based can be both exciting and alluring. Many agents, including those who are brand new to the industry, believe that a big deal is right around the corner.

The truth is that the key to their success is hard work and diligent planning. It can often take years to build your business, and you must be driven by an entrepreneurial spirit and a real fire in your belly throughout your career.

If I could change one thing in the industry, it might be to set up some sort of periodic litmus test for agents, perhaps at key stages in their careers, to evaluate their continued readiness to work as hard as they must to remain relevant so it continues to be financially viable for them long term.

How have your expectations of your management team changed over the past two years?

The responsibilities of our executives have become far more comprehensive over the past years. Their jobs now involve so much beyond managing expectations, being a deal doctor and helping agents develop and keep their goals on track. As a result, we expect our executives to be extremely well-rounded.

In addition to their more traditional roles, we take a lot of pride in the fact that our executives maintain and embody our collaborative company culture—both within the office and by fostering connections between our agents outside the office—as well as develop deep expertise in our technology and help lead the implementation of it.

Our executives are also constantly networking for new talent as well as acting as a ready ear for agents' personal and business issues. It is important to us that they not only wear but thrive in wearing many hats.

How do you keep your team competitive?

It is so important that we mirror for our executive team the support they provide to our agents. Everything our executives do for the agents—listen, collaborate, support, mentor and celebrate—we do for them so they have the confidence and the ability to go the extra mile to ensure we are at the top of our game for our agents and as a firm.

With so much disruption in real estate, what's your best advice for managing change?

Lean into change. Real estate has always been a constantly evolving industry, and this continues to push us to new heights. Change will always be an important part of the business. Our agents help people make changes and transitions at each critical stage in their lives. And as the brokerage community, we must view innovations within our industry as positive things that will keep us on our toes and, more importantly, empower us to help clients make improvements in their own lives.

At Halstead, an important foundation of our culture is not just a willingness but a true desire to embrace this kind of change. We are always ready and searching for new tools and ideas that will make us a better company for our agents and clients; it's not simply change—it's innovation.

28.

Leadership Lens: It's an awesome time for our industry

Daniel Dannenmann

We recently sat down with Daniel Dannenmann, president at Better Homes and Gardens Real Estate Bradfield Properties in San Antonio, Texas, to understand his thoughts and insights on the current state of real estate leadership, how he manages change and disruption with his team, and how he maintains his company's competitive edge.

As a leader, what keeps you up at night?

A loaded question really: "What will my 8-year-old daughter's path through life look like," is the honest answer. But that is not what you are looking for …

So in all things real estate, what truly keeps me up is to figure out how I make enough time in the day to test all new thoughts and technologies that are (finally) appearing in real estate.

It's an awesome time for our industry. It's a time when new operation models and new tech solutions flood in seemingly by the day. For me it's not the "what-haven't-I seen" or "what-haven't-I-tried" thoughts that won't let me sleep at night, but rather thoughts around how to keep my teams focused and my agents engaged.

I view it as my task as a leader to keep them "out" of the tech-and-options jungle. It is my task to show them the paths that I want them to engage on and to be brilliant at. Thus, sleepless nights for me are all about wondering whether those who work with me can keep their focus and their execution.

If you could change one thing in real estate, what would it be?

Hard to have my brain go only one way when I think about true gamechangers for the industry. Since I have a "left side" and "right side," I will go both ways:

Right side: Consolidation of all multiple listing services (MLSs) into a few (5-10) key regional players. Life would be infinitely simpler ...

Left side: Our industry adopts higher standards for becoming a Realtor and, consequently, adopts a "base salary + commissions" approach. The amount of talent we would be able to draw would be staggering.

How have your expectations of your management team changed over the past 2 years?

Truthfully, not much. (I surprise myself.)

I expect my management team to be able to:

1. Keep a pulse on the market (*their* market and the industry).

2. Come to me with ideas that consistently improve us (or in the best case are the birthplace for new BHAGREs).

3. Keep close track of all key operational Performance Indicators in their respective offices or regions.

What has changed however is the amount of influx of new ideas as well as our ability to mine data (our own or purchased) in many new and meaningful ways. One new skill level that has developed over the last years as a result is the required ability to run a true beta test of systems and process, evaluate results and report back conclusively to enable meaningful action at the company level.

It turns out that "testing stuff" is not that easy.

Thus, what continues to be of mounting importance is our need to communicate with each other to ensure we stay on the same track.

How do you keep your team competitive?

Clean direction: Communicate the vision for our company in an unmistakable way. Everyone needs to know what our "North Star" is.

Independence: Framed by our vision and BHGRE's, I encourage free idea flow. No idea is too big or too "out there" to talk about. Only when we look at the seemingly crazy or unreachable do we start to stretch.

In the last three months, that has resulted in building a video game for Talent Attraction and in building an MLS agent scraper that allows us to get key agent-level data, even in markets that do not consolidate to a Terradatum product.

Our task for innovation continues as we are half way down the line of building "Brad," our own artificial intelligence (AI) chatbot, initially focused on helping our agents find the answers they need.

Talent: Perhaps the most significant change of recent years in real estate is the need for new and different talent in the organization. Upgrading our human resources with colleagues that bring true technical capability (both in strategy and coding) to the table is critical in maintaining a competitive edge.

With so much disruption in real estate, what's your best advice for managing change?

I am not sure if there is *one* best advice I have. I would have to settle for (at least) two:

Stay calm. Seriously. Not obtuse, but calm in the face of new opportunity.

Innovation and disruption is going on not just in real estate but in every industry. Just think about the pace of innovation in technology or in medicine … it's mind-boggling!

The worst thing we all can do as leaders is to cry "gold" or "doom" every time we see a new and shiny thing. Evaluate the options, technologies and ideas you see, carefully stitch together what works for you and then … *execute relentlessly*.

Success is in the execution, not in merely having ideas. And certainly not in panicking. Stay calm. Educate yourself. Develop a vision. Onboard the talent you need. Communicate. Execute. *Lead*.

Don't change for the sake of change. Don't change because you feel it's the cool thing to do.

Change is a tool; it is *not* a goal itself. Remember the core principles of managing change and act by them. The most critical element of change is for us as leaders to be able to clearly define a desired future state. Then put together the pieces that get you there. *Calmly*.

29.

Leadership Lens: Consolidate the MLS!

James Dwiggins

James Dwiggins is the chief executive officer at NextHome, Inc., a progressive real estate franchise with consumer-focused branding, technology and marketing. NextHome focuses on collaborative partnerships and effective products for business development, growth and relevance.

We recently had the opportunity to sit down with James and pick his brain about his perspective on the future of real estate leadership.

As a leader, what keeps you up at night?

The realization that our industry as a whole truly does not understand who their customer is and what they want in a real estate buying or selling experience.

Our industry has been so slow to change to consumer demands, I simply do not see a future anymore within the next five to 10 years where the agent population hasn't been reduced to half its current level. The lack of brokerage minimum standards, agent oversight and service level has created an environment where most consumers truly don't understand what our industry provides for the fees it charges.

This is one of the main drivers behind all the venture capital (VC) pouring into real estate. Consumers think our industry charges too much and provides little value in return—and in many cases, it's true.

We've all heard the stories from friends and family about these bad real estate experiences all too often. And frankly, when most brokerages continue to focus their agents attention on fees, splits, revenue share, etc., versus whatever it takes to increase their consumer value proposition, you know they're either oblivious to the reality they're facing or are choosing to ignore it.

Every real estate broker and agent must be heavily focused on how their brand is perceived in the market, and making sure their marketing, their service level, their advertising and their technology are all clearly understood and valued by today's consumer.

Everything needs to be about making sure consumers want to choose them versus going it alone or using an alternative business model like Opendoor, OfferPad, RoofStock or even discount models like Redfin or Purplebricks. These companies are not going away and have significant money to compete and take market share. They're already doing it!

It's amazing to me that most leadership teams are focused on commission splits and technology to recruit/retain agents as a way to stay relevant. My biggest fear is that leadership in most real estate brokerages, and franchisors, are not changing fast enough. We continue to have conversations about compensation without getting real estate company leadership focused on the right things.

If you could change one thing in real estate, what would it be?

Consolidate all the multiple listing services (MLSs) down to 50 statewide systems. The amount of money it would save franchisors, brokerages, agents and technology companies wanting to build amazing products for our industry would be substantial. The only reason we're not there is politics and brokerages/agents not forcing these mergers to happen faster. This should have occurred long ago.

How have your expectations of your management team changed over the past two years?

They haven't. I'm truly blessed to have the opportunity to work with some of the brightest minds in the business. From day one, we started NextHome with the goal of making our brokerages and agents the central and most important part of every real estate transaction for consumers.

Everything we do is built around what buyers and sellers want from their agents and a real estate buying or selling experience. Never have we been more focused on that core mission than today. Our team is very passionate about it, and we push each other and our members to be better each and every day.

How do you keep your team competitive?

We go into every conversation or meeting looking for the best idea or ways to make any idea great. There are no egos allowed—it's that simple.

Our team is extremely passionate about achieving the goals we set each year and, more importantly, making sure our members love working with us, and their clients love working with them.

We want to see this great profession succeed into the future and have the real estate agent reputation be known as a professional one. That's all the competition we need.

With so much disruption in real estate, what's your best advice for managing change?

Focus on the consumer. Get a group of buyers and sellers together who are willing to give you honest feedback on anything you're trying or thinking of implementing.

Embrace change. Make it part of your company culture and who you are. Get rid of people who fight it, and bring in people who love it.

Make sure your primary goal is to increase the value proposition of your brokerage and what you provide your agents. They are your voice to consumers and if they don't have an amazing value proposition and experience to provide, you (and they) will ultimately fail.

Change is hard—it's the thing we fear most. However, if you create a safe environment where people learn to love it, you will succeed in the long run.

30.

Leadership Lens: Investing in a singular goal

David Marine

David Marine

David Marine is the senior vice president of brand engagement for Coldwell Banker, where he positively influences consumers on a mass scale from his management of world-class, award-winning advertising campaigns to elevating Coldwell Banker's digital footprint each year with his creativity in regard to content and video creation, which has garnered over 60 million viewers in 2016 alone.

As team leader for Coldwell Banker's consumer and network engagement, he is mentoring and grooming a team of digital natives who attribute their own success directly to what they have learned from David.

David has had a profound impact in the real estate industry in each of his 13 years at Coldwell Banker and somehow continues to raise an already recording setting bar of excellence to new heights with each year that passes.

We recently sat down with David to chat about the future of real estate leadership.

As a leader, what keeps you up at night?

Failure. A simple and obvious answer, but it can come in many forms, from complacency to inability to anticipate change to poor execution.

If you could change one thing in real estate, what would it be?

How we handle our data. Given the amount of data out there being transacted every single day, it's still amazing to me that we don't have better data insights, reporting structures and analysis reporting than other industries.

How have your expectations of your management team changed over the past two years?

There's a greater expectation for the whole team to be fully invested in a singular goal. Previously, each group had something they were focused on, but that focus wasn't necessarily the same as the focus of the person next to them.

Today, we have everyone focused on the same metric for success, which not only helps build the business but strengthens the team as well.

How do you keep your team competitive?

My team has an innate competitive nature that keeps us motivated, but we also like to look at how we compare within our industry and outside it.

We're not satisfied with just meeting the performance standard of our direct competition. As a leader of a national brand, we find inspiration and motivation from looking outside as well.

With so much disruption in real estate, what's your best advice for managing change?

Transparency. It may sound cliché, but being transparent and open with communication and changes is the best thing that's helped me manage through change.

31.

Leadership Lens: Cultivate change before it's trending

Caroline Pinal

Fueled by a passion for social entrepreneurship, Caroline Pinal helped create Giveback Homes to empower real estate agents to turn their everyday business into an opportunity for social change. Caroline and her team deliver innovation and impact to their network of like-minded agents, which are the driving force behind the movement to provide safe homes for families throughout the world. We had the opportunity to ask Caroline for her thoughts on the future of real estate leadership.

As a leader, what keeps you up at night?

The global housing crisis can feel insurmountable at times, and at the same time I think a lot about how to balance the ongoing needs in communities we serve with mobilizing responses to current events and how to better prepare the companies we work with to assist.

If you could change one thing in real estate, what would it be?

I wish all real estate developers in the entire world were required to build affordable housing solutions into each project.

How have your expectations of your management team changed over the past two years?

Two years ago, the expectation was to do everything, be everything, to everyone 24/7. Today, the expectation is to stay focused on our members and partners and what we're aiming to do next. Reminding ourselves what we're not doing is equally important. This has made it easy to say no to certain things, resulting in less distractions and better service to our people.

How do you keep your team competitive?

The no. 1 question we get asked is, "how much do other people typically give?" and I used to think this is such a strange question. But I've learned that people are more likely to give more, if they know the amount that their peers/colleagues are giving. And often the amount that people donate is related to how much they believe others are donating.

It's naturally competitive, but ultimately the more people that give, the more everyone wins. That's why it's important to share how and who is giving, because it will always inspire others to give in one way or another.

With so much disruption in real estate, what's your best advice for managing change?

Cultivate change before it's a trending topic. Your enthusiasm will always be the driving force behind whether something is successful or not.

32.

Leadership Lens: Sherry Chris on picking a swim lane and sticking to it

Sherry Chris

Sherry Chris

Sherry Chris, the Chief Executive Officer and President of Better Homes and Gardens Real Estate is a seasoned executive with over 30 years of experience in real estate, technology and franchising. Her current venture is overseeing and driving growth for Realogy's newest growth brand, Better Homes and Gardens Real Estate.

She enjoys giving back to the industry by serving on various boards and committees as well as sharing best practices and challenging the status quo, and is passionate about giving back to those less fortunate. In 10 years Better Homes and Gardens Real Estate has grown into 39 states, three countries with 350 offices and more than 11,000 agents. We recently had the opportunity to sit down with Sherry and pick her brain about the future of real estate leadership.

As a leader, what keeps you up at night?

Continuing to provide exceptional customer service to our franchisees and agents so they can build valuable business assets. Also, working to enhance the customer experience so the joy of moving on to the next phase of your life from a real estate perspective is memorable. In a nutshell – exceeding expectations on all fronts. That is how you keep ahead of the game.

If you could change one thing in real estate, what would it be?

That we all respect one another and work together as human beings to make this industry a better place, and ultimately provide a higher level of service to the end consumer.

How have your expectations of your management team changed over the past two years?

I continue to empower my team to make a difference, find a better way. Surprise and delight. That has not and will not change.

How do you keep your team competitive?

I challenge my team to execute on all of my "unusual" ideas or convince me why they should not. That pretty much sums up our day to day experience at BHGRE

With so much disruption in real estate, what's your best advice for managing change?

Pick a swim lane, stick to it, be the best in your lane.

33.

Leadership Lens: Work on being indispensable

Denee Evans

Denee Evans

Denee Evans is the CEO at Council of Multiple Listing Services. A distinguished executive who is passionate about strengthening communities through finance, innovation, and technology, she has applied a broad range of financial expertise, program development experience, and leadership skills to accomplish this objective by transforming departments, offices, and organizations into peak performing operations that have a direct impact in our communities. We recently had the chance to sit down with Denee and ask her thoughts on the future of real estate leadership in 2018.

As a leader, what keeps you up at night?

The real estate industry tends to pour so much effort into today's problems that there never seems to be anything left for tomorrow. So I'm constantly looking for that one compelling case—that one defining vision—that can persuade the entire industry to stop hunting for the next disruption and start investing in the creation of something better. Don't worry about being relevant today. Start working to be indispensable tomorrow.

If you could change one thing in real estate, what would it be?

I would bring all the stakeholders together and channel their energy toward a collaborative effort that leads to something better—a marketplace that is intuitive to the needs of consumers, provided by brokers, served by agents, and connected by MLSs. This might make some people uncomfortable, but that's a good thing. Operating outside your comfort zone is often the first step toward success.

How have your expectations of your management team changed over the past two years?

At the Council of MLS, I work with different management teams that are growing all the time. I've seen the CMLS Board of Directors evolve from a tactical one that asks "what now?" to a strategic one that asks "what if?" I've built a dedicated full-time staff that eats, sleeps, and breathes MLS in order to better support our members. And as a result of their efforts, the expectations of the industry are starting to change so we can begin to explore what the real possibilities might be.

How do you keep your team competitive?

As a trade organization representing the MLS community, this question requires a different kind of answer. It's really less about direct competition and more about delivering value as an indispensable resource that makes our MLS members the ones that everyone else aspires to be. I want them to be the MLSs that define service excellence, develop best practices, and are recognized as best-in-class organizations.

With so much disruption in real estate, what's your best
advice for managing change?

The time has come for MLSs to stop managing the change and
start making the change. You don't have to worry about disruption
when you are one of the leaders contributing to a better marketplace. Let's inspire the industry to reimagine tomorrow's marketplace in ways that make sense. Since change is inevitable, let's
collaborate with those who are seen as its architects. We're working at this every day at CMLS, inspiring not only ourselves but
everyone we work with along the way.

Inman Survey: What does the real estate industry want from its leaders?

Q1 What qualities do you think are most important for good leadership? (Check all that apply.)

Answered: 787   Skipped: 0

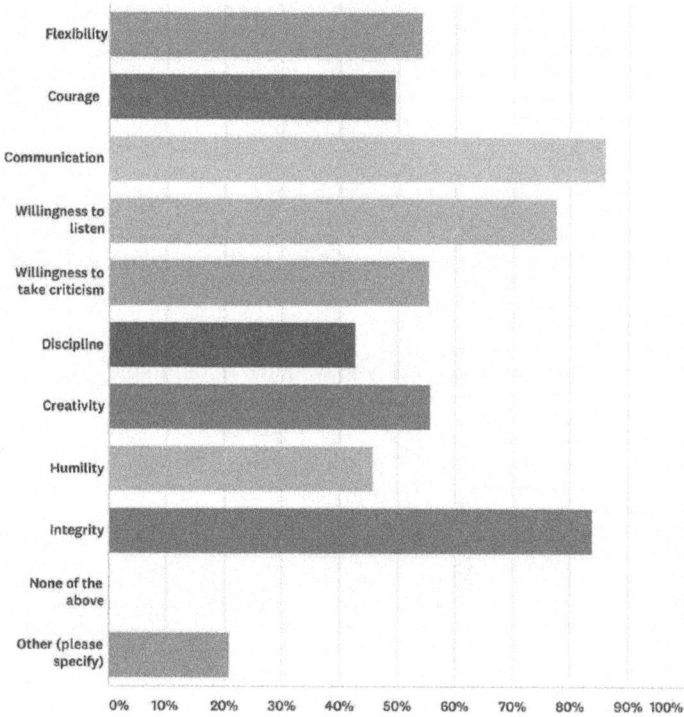

ANSWER CHOICES	RESPONSES	
Flexibility	54.13%	426
Courage	49.68%	391
Communication	85.90%	676
Willingness to listen	77.64%	611
Willingness to take criticism	55.53%	437
Discipline	42.69%	336
Creativity	55.65%	438
Humility	45.74%	360
Integrity	83.86%	660

Q2 Do your leader(s) know you by your name and what job you do?

Answered: 787   Skipped: 0

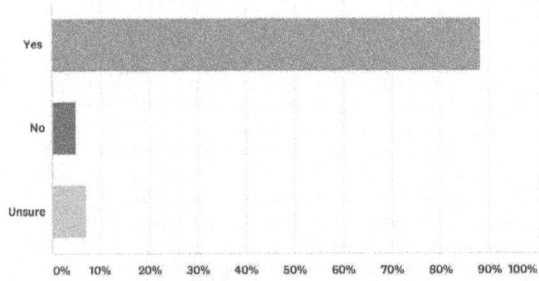

ANSWER CHOICES	RESPONSES	
Yes	88.18%	694
No	4.83%	38
Unsure	6.99%	55
TOTAL		787

Q4 How happy are you with the leadership of your company?

Answered: 787   Skipped: 0

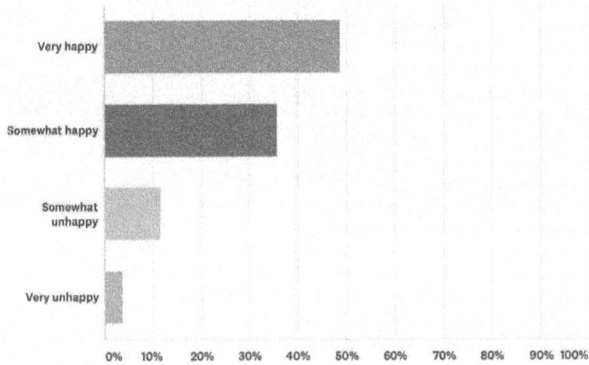

ANSWER CHOICES	RESPONSES	
Very happy	48.79%	384
Somewhat happy	35.71%	281
Somewhat unhappy	11.82%	93
Very unhappy	3.68%	29
TOTAL		787

Q6 Which of the following best describes the hierarchy structure of your company?

Answered: 787   Skipped: 0

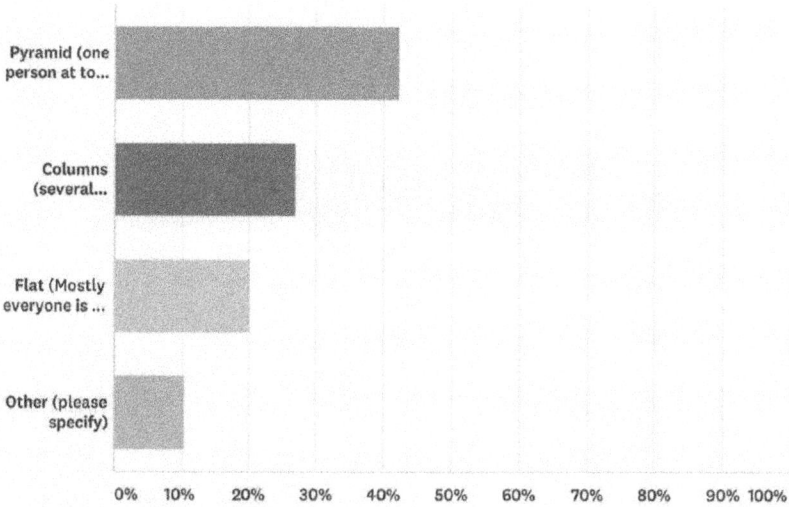

ANSWER CHOICES	RESPONSES	
Pyramid (one person at top, several layers of management below them)	42.19%	332
Columns (several divisions with positions of equal levels reporting up to a single leader or board)	27.06%	213
Flat (Mostly everyone is on the same level)	20.33%	160
Other (please specify)	10.42%	82
TOTAL		787

Q7 How are workers at your company compensated? (Check all that apply.)

Answered: 787   Skipped: 0

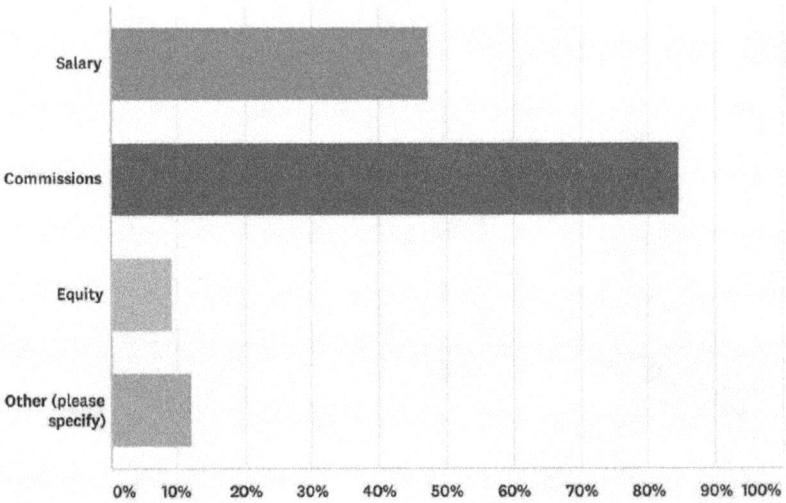

ANSWER CHOICES	RESPONSES	
Salary	47.27%	372
Commissions	84.50%	665
Equity	9.15%	72
Other (please specify)	12.07%	95
Total Respondents: 787		

Q8 What are the biggest problems at your company that leadership is not addressing? (Check all that apply.)

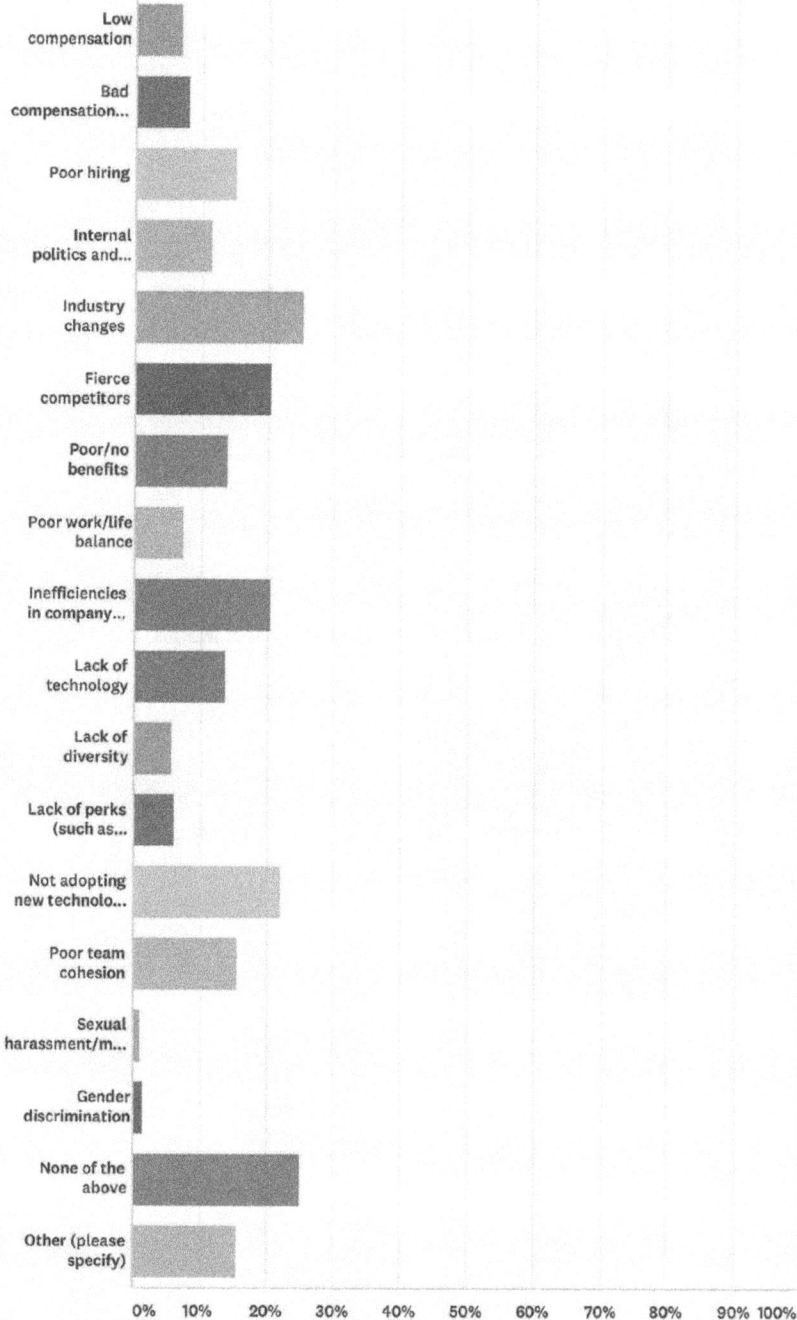

ANSWER CHOICES	RESPONSES	
Low compensation	6.99%	55
Bad compensation structure	7.88%	62
Poor hiring	15.37%	121
Internal politics and infighting	11.56%	91
Industry changes	25.29%	199
Fierce competitors	20.58%	162
Poor/no benefits	14.10%	111
Poor work/life balance	7.24%	57
Inefficiencies in company structure	20.58%	162
Lack of technology	13.85%	109
Lack of diversity	5.59%	44
Lack of perks (such as coffee, supplies)	5.97%	47
Not adopting new technology fast enough	22.24%	175
Poor team cohesion	15.63%	123
Sexual harassment/misconduct	1.14%	9
Gender discrimination	1.40%	11
None of the above	25.16%	198
Other (please specify)	15.76%	124
Total Respondents: 787		

Q10 How technologically literate is your leadership?

Answered: 787   Skipped: 0

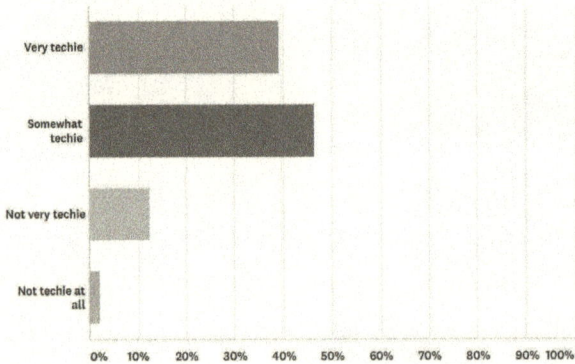

ANSWER CHOICES	RESPONSES	
Very techie	39.14%	308
Somewhat techie	46.38%	365
Not very techie	12.33%	97
Not techie at all	2.16%	17
TOTAL		787

Q11 Which of the following tech trends or practices has your leadership pushed your organization to adopt? (Check all that apply.)

Answered: 787   Skipped: 0

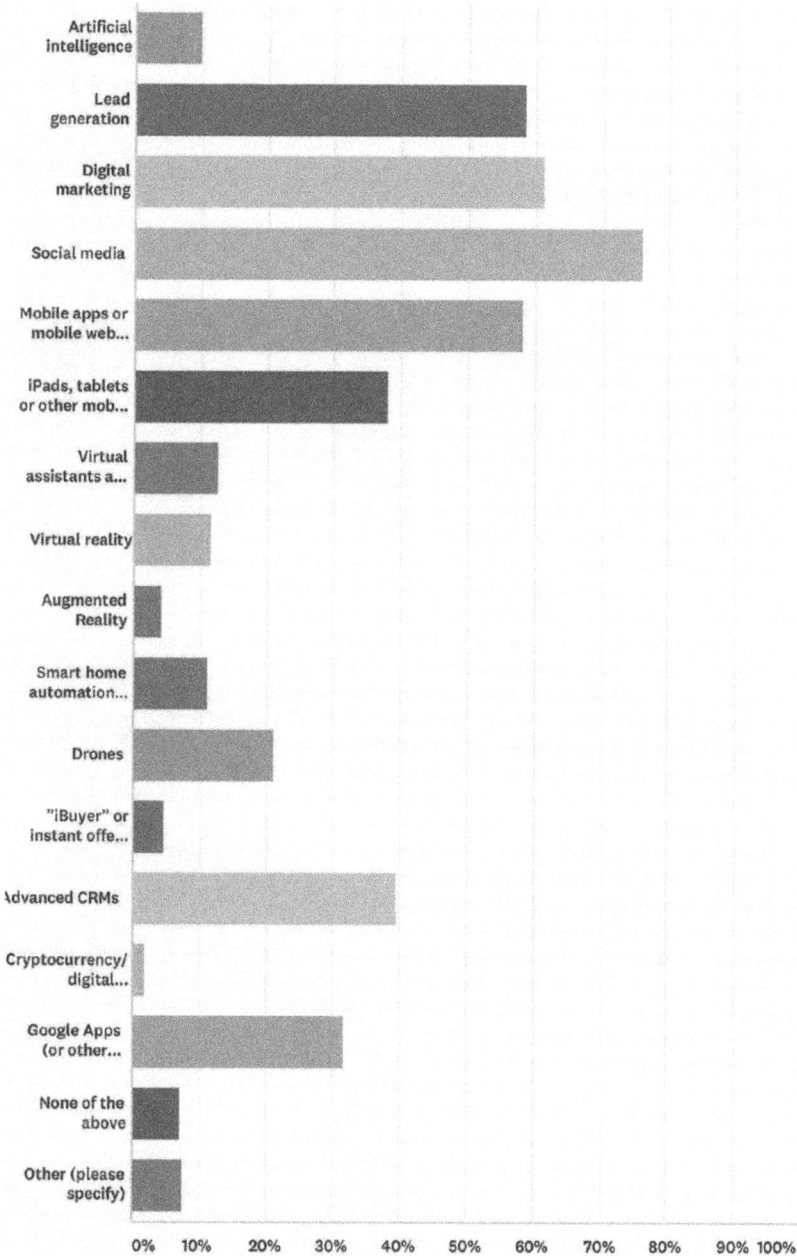

ANSWER CHOICES	RESPONSES	
Artificial intelligence	9.91%	78
Lead generation	58.58%	461
Digital marketing	61.25%	482
Social media	75.86%	597
Mobile apps or mobile web interfaces	58.07%	457
iPads, tablets or other mobile devices	38.12%	300
Virtual assistants and smart speakers (e.g. Amazon Alexa)	12.45%	98
Virtual reality	11.56%	91
Augmented Reality	4.19%	33
Smart home automation (e.g. Nest and smart locks)	11.05%	87
Drones	21.22%	167
"iBuyer" or instant offer technology	4.70%	37
Advanced CRMs	39.52%	311
Cryptocurrency/digital currency token payments	1.78%	14
Google Apps (or other cloud-based software)	31.89%	251
None of the above	7.12%	56
Other (please specify)	7.62%	60
Total Respondents: 787		

Q12 What new tools should your company's leadership be using that they don't currently? (Check all that apply.)

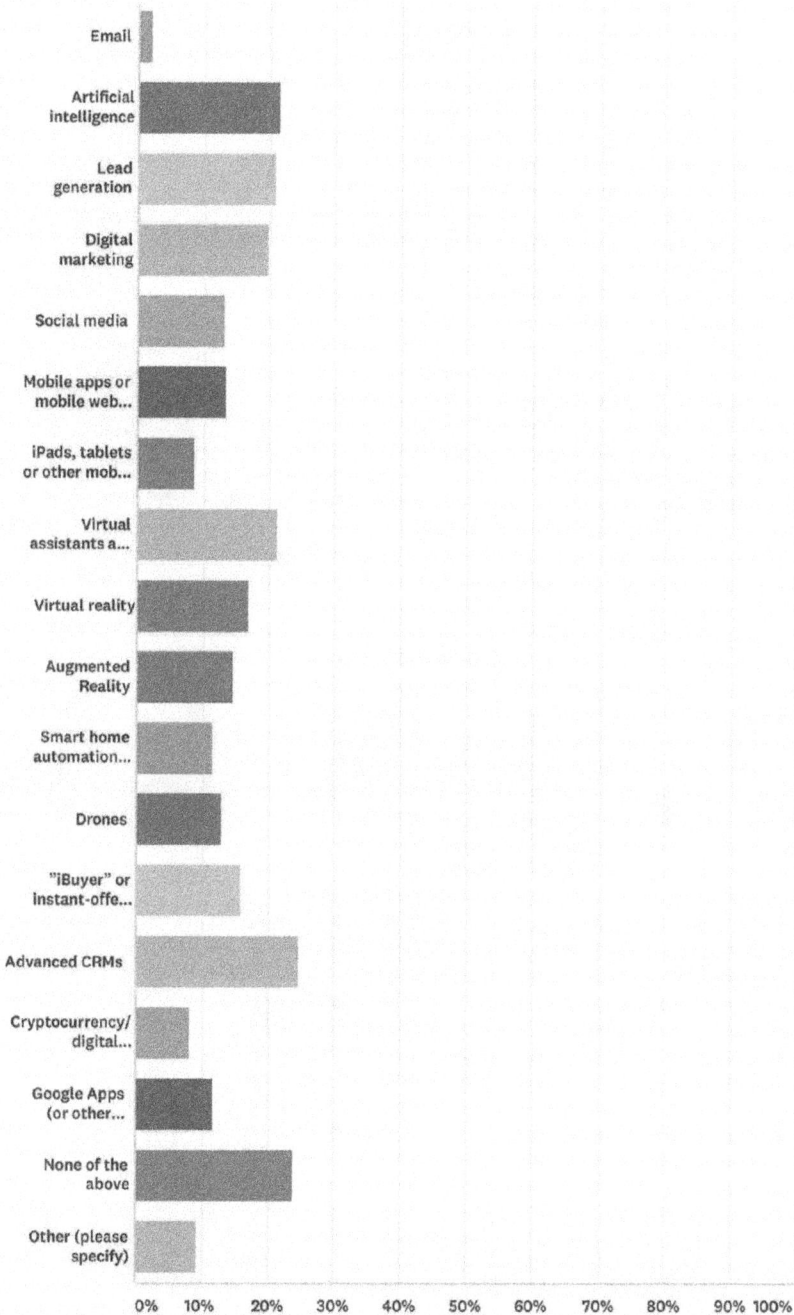

ANSWER CHOICES	RESPONSES	
Email	2.03%	16
Artificial intelligence	21.47%	169
Lead generation	20.84%	164
Digital marketing	19.82%	156
Social media	13.21%	104
Mobile apps or mobile web interfaces	13.34%	105
iPads, tablets or other mobile devices	8.64%	68
Virtual assistants and smart speakers (e.g. Amazon Alexa)	21.35%	168
Virtual reality	16.90%	133
Augmented Reality	14.74%	116
Smart home automation (e.g. Nest and smart locks)	11.44%	90
Drones	12.96%	102
"iBuyer" or instant-offer technology	15.88%	125
Advanced CRMs	24.65%	194
Cryptocurrency/digital currency token payments	8.26%	65
Google Apps (or other cloud-based software)	11.69%	92
None of the above	23.89%	188
Other (please specify)	9.15%	72
Total Respondents: 787		

Q13 How would you characterize your leaders' commitments to workplace diversity?

Answered: 787   Skipped: 0

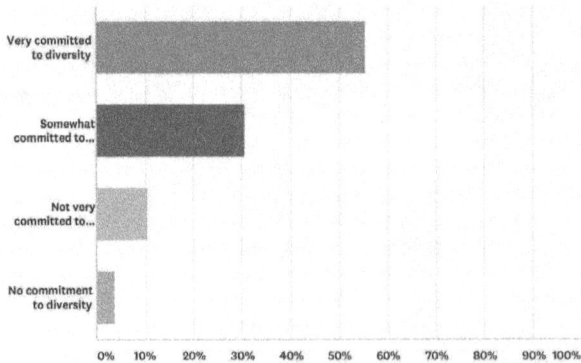

ANSWER CHOICES	RESPONSES	
Very committed to diversity	55.40%	436
Somewhat committed to diversity	30.50%	240
Not very committed to diversity	10.42%	82
No commitment to diversity	3.68%	29
TOTAL		787

Q14 Do you want your leaders to be more committed to diversity?

Answered: 787   Skipped: 0

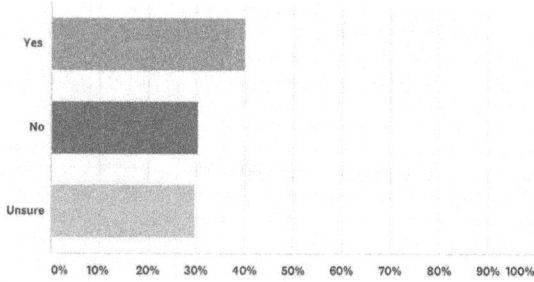

ANSWER CHOICES	RESPONSES	
Yes	40.03%	315
No	30.37%	239
Unsure	29.61%	233
TOTAL		787

Q15 Does your leadership support hires of all age groups, or do they tend to favor hires of a certain age group?

Answered: 787   Skipped: 0

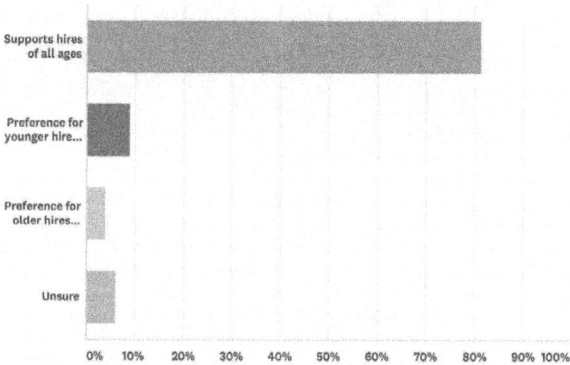

ANSWER CHOICES	RESPONSES	
Supports hires of all ages	81.19%	639
Preference for younger hires (20s and 30s)	8.89%	70
Preference for older hires (middle-age and above)	3.94%	31
Unsure	5.97%	47
TOTAL		787

Q16 How would you characterize your company's position on sexual harassment or other forms of sexual misconduct in the workplace?

Answered: 787   Skipped: 0

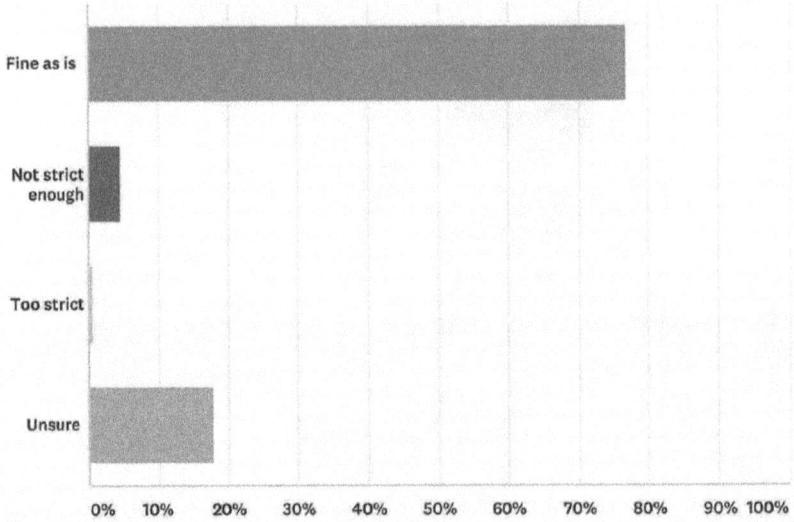

ANSWER CHOICES	RESPONSES	
Fine as is	76.75%	604
Not strict enough	4.70%	37
Too strict	0.64%	5
Unsure	17.92%	141
TOTAL		787

Q17 How would you characterize your leaders' frequency of communication with you?

Answered: 787   Skipped: 0

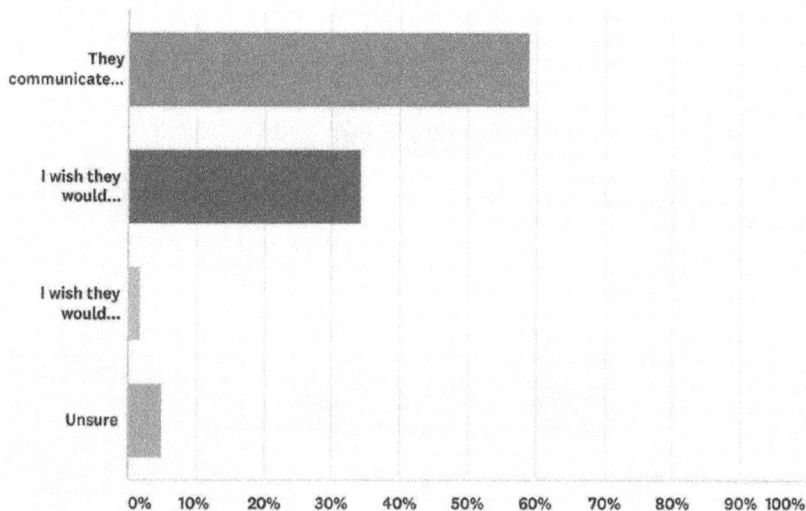

ANSWER CHOICES	RESPONSES	
They communicate with me just enough	58.96%	464
I wish they would communicate with me more	34.31%	270
I wish they would communicate with me less	1.78%	14
Unsure	4.96%	39
TOTAL		787

Q18 What methods of communication do you want your leaders to be using to reach you? (Check all that apply.)

Answered: 787   Skipped: 0

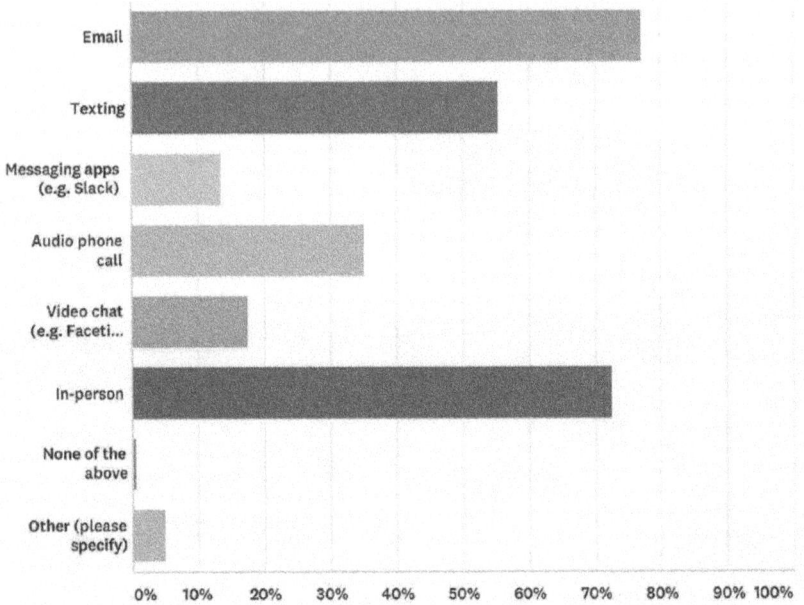

ANSWER CHOICES	RESPONSES	
Email	77.13%	607
Texting	55.53%	437
Messaging apps (e.g. Slack)	13.60%	107
Audio phone call	35.20%	277
Video chat (e.g. Facetime or Google Hangouts)	17.53%	138
In-person	72.68%	572
None of the above	0.64%	5
Other (please specify)	4.96%	39
Total Respondents: 787		

Q19 If you're an agent/independent contractor, do you have access to affordable health care?

Answered: 758   Skipped: 29

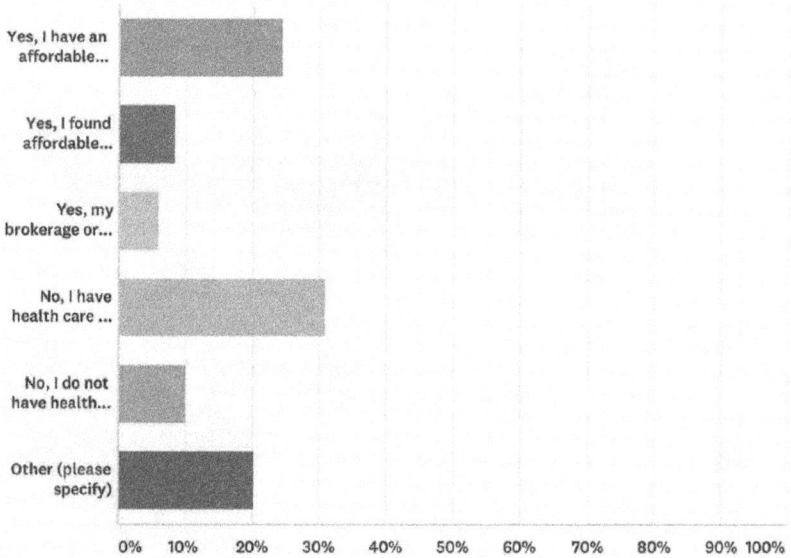

ANSWER CHOICES	RESPONSES	
Yes, I have an affordable health plan through my spouse	24.41%	185
Yes, I found affordable health care on the exchange	8.44%	64
Yes, my brokerage or association provides me access to affordable healthcare	5.80%	44
No, I have health care but it is not affordable	31.00%	235
No, I do not have health insurance	10.03%	76
Other (please specify)	20.32%	154
TOTAL		758

Q20 Does the leadership of your company engage in inappropriate behavior?

Answered: 787   Skipped: 0

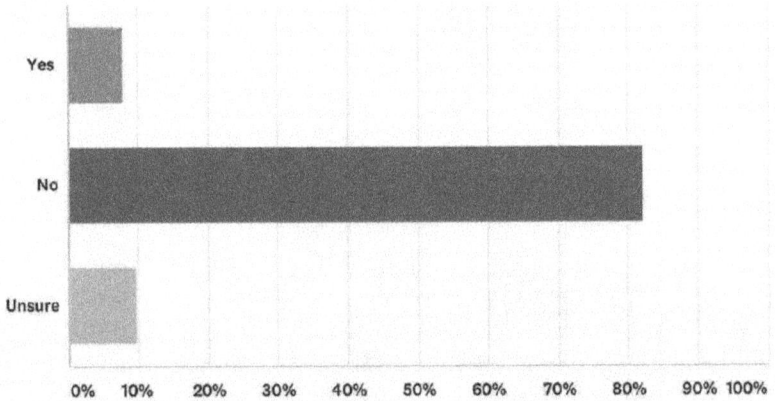

ANSWER CHOICES	RESPONSES	
Yes	7.88%	62
No	82.21%	647
Unsure	9.91%	78
TOTAL		787

Q22 What are the age ranges of your company's leaders? (Check all that apply.)

Answered: 787   Skipped: 0

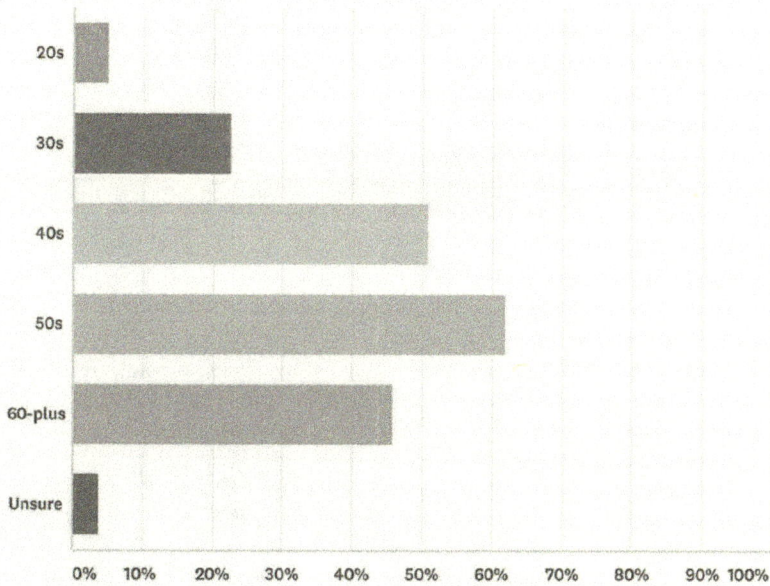

ANSWER CHOICES	RESPONSES	
20s	5.08%	40
30s	22.62%	178
40s	50.83%	400
50s	62.01%	488
60-plus	45.87%	361
Unsure	3.68%	29
Total Respondents: 787		

Q23 Which of the following best describes your company's leadership style?

Answered: 787   Skipped: 0

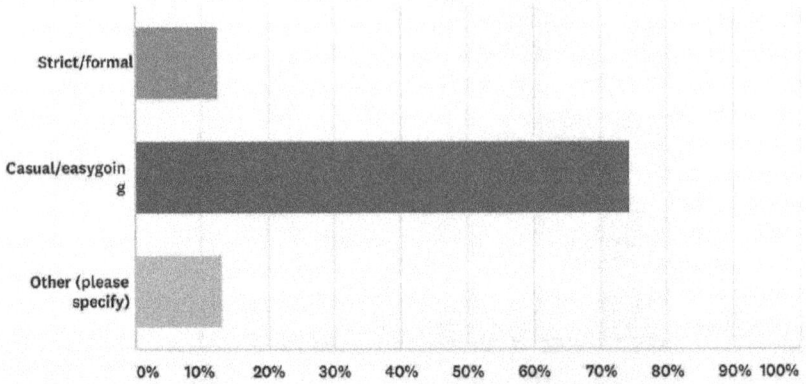

ANSWER CHOICES	RESPONSES	
Strict/formal	12.45%	98
Casual/easygoing	74.46%	586
Other (please specify)	13.09%	103
TOTAL		787

Q24 If your leadership could improve itself in one area, what would it be? (Check one.)

Answered: 787   Skipped: 0

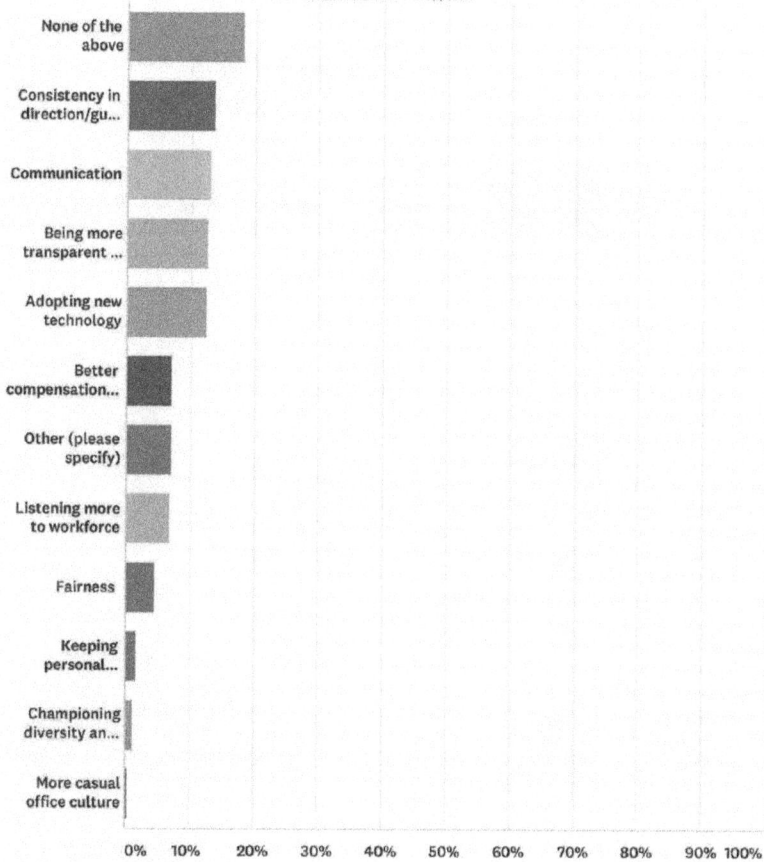

ANSWER CHOICES	RESPONSES	
None of the above	18.17%	143
Consistency in direction/guidance	13.85%	109
Communication	13.21%	104
Being more transparent in decision-making and thinking	12.83%	101
Adopting new technology	12.58%	99
Better compensation for employees	7.12%	56
Other (please specify)	7.12%	56
Listening more to workforce	6.99%	55
Fairness	4.70%	37
Keeping personal politics/beliefs at home	1.65%	13
Championing diversity and other social causes	1.27%	10
More casual office culture	0.51%	4
TOTAL		787

Q25 If you are a solo real estate practitioner, is industry leadership something you even think about?

Answered: 682   Skipped: 105

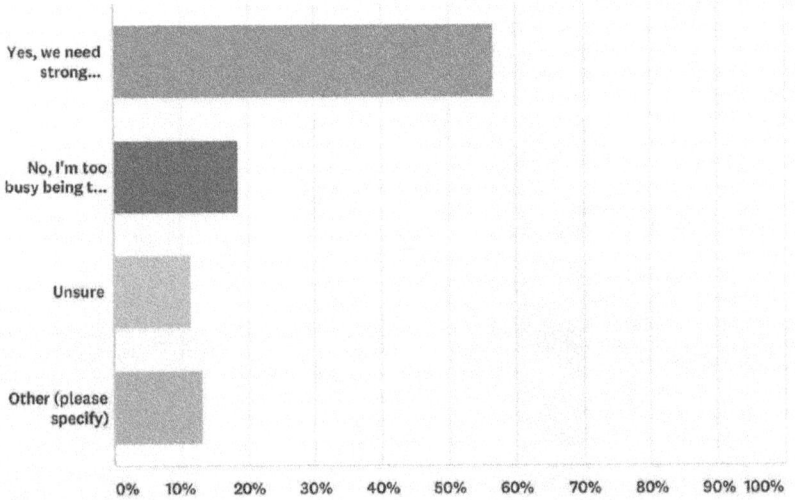

ANSWER CHOICES	RESPONSES	
Yes, we need strong leadership to navigate real estate's future	56.60%	386
No, I'm too busy being the captain of my own destiny	18.62%	127
Unsure	11.58%	79
Other (please specify)	13.20%	90
TOTAL		682

Q26 How much does your leadership work with experts outside your business (and outside the industry)?

Answered: 787   Skipped: 0

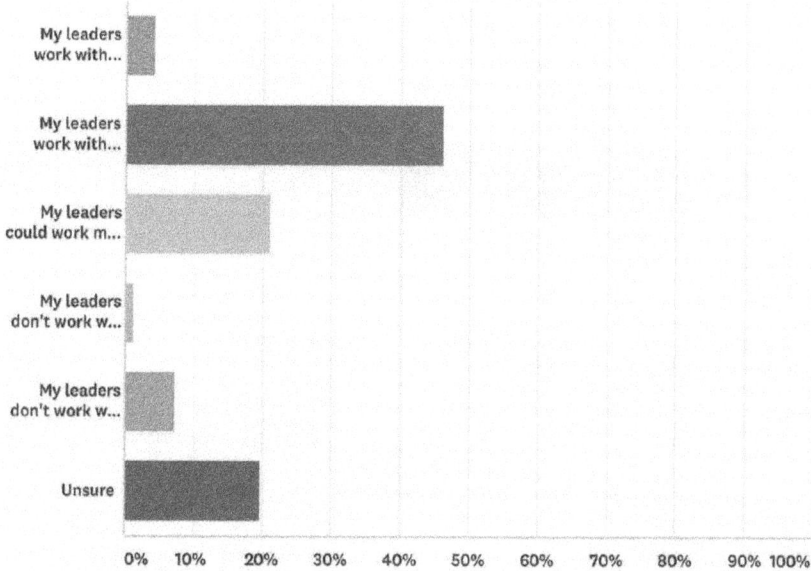

ANSWER CHOICES	RESPONSES	
My leaders work with outside experts too much	4.19%	33
My leaders work with outside experts just the right amount	46.25%	364
My leaders could work more with outside experts	21.22%	167
My leaders don't work with outside experts at all, and that's how it should be	1.27%	10
My leaders don't work with outside experts at all, and I wish they would	7.24%	57
Unsure	19.82%	156
TOTAL		787

Q27 How well do you think your leadership handles challenges to your business?

Answered: 774   Skipped: 13

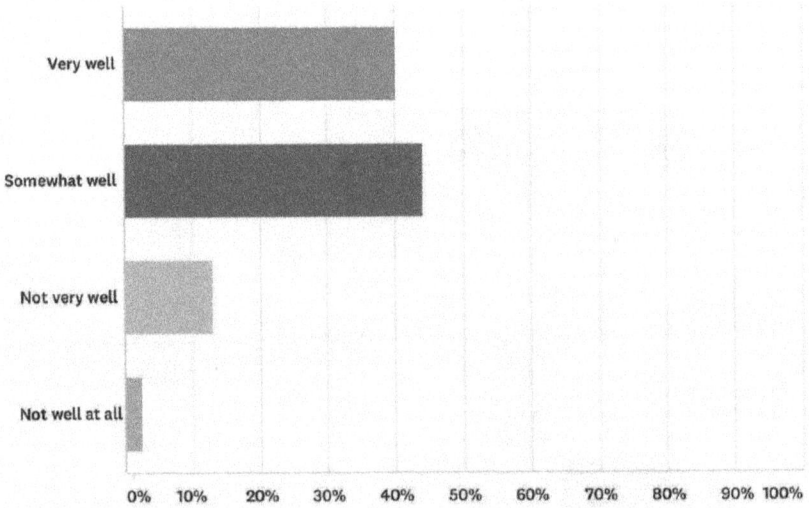

ANSWER CHOICES	RESPONSES	
Very well	40.18%	311
Somewhat well	44.06%	341
Not very well	13.18%	102
Not well at all	2.58%	20
TOTAL		774

Q28 What are the biggest industry challenges that your leadership is failing to address? (Check all that apply.)

Answered: 774   Skipped: 13

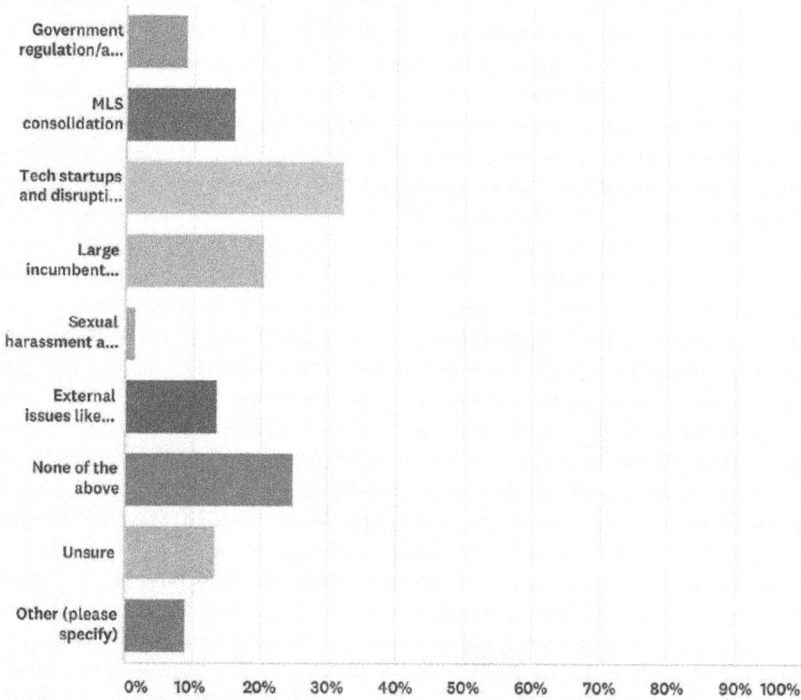

ANSWER CHOICES	RESPONSES	
Government regulation/antitrust	8.91%	69
MLS consolidation	16.15%	125
Tech startups and disruptive new technology	32.30%	250
Large incumbent companies absorbing more market share	20.54%	159
Sexual harassment and sexual misconduct	1.42%	11
External issues like affordable housing, climate change or economic issues	13.57%	105
None of the above	24.81%	192
Unsure	13.31%	103
Other (please specify)	9.04%	70
Total Respondents: 774		

Q29 What companies and organizations in the industry do you think have exemplary leadership? (Check all that apply.)

Answered: 774   Skipped: 13

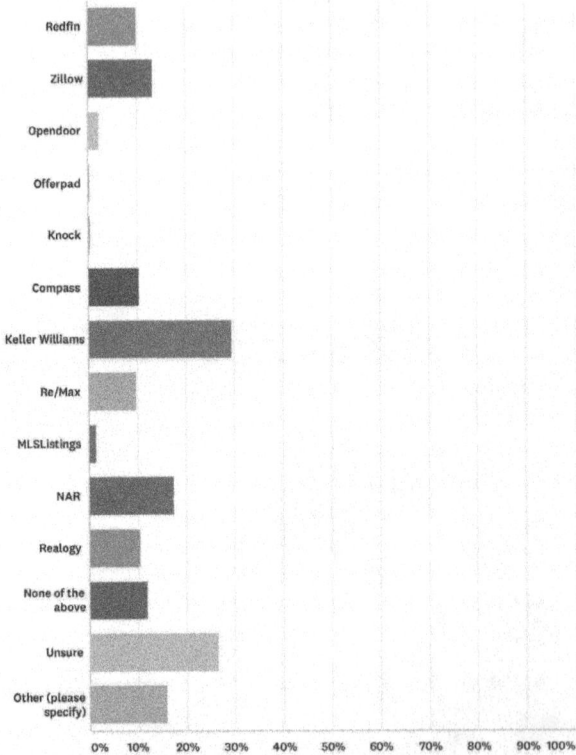

ANSWER CHOICES	RESPONSES	
Redfin	10.08%	78
Zillow	13.44%	104
Opendoor	2.33%	18
Offerpad	0.52%	4
Knock	0.39%	3
Compass	10.47%	81
Keller Williams	29.59%	229
Re/Max	9.82%	76
MLSListings	1.42%	11
NAR	17.57%	136
Realogy	10.47%	81
None of the above	11.89%	92
Unsure	26.49%	205
Other (please specify)	15.89%	123
Total Respondents: 774		

Q30 Which companies do you think are lacking in good leadership? (Check all that apply.)

Answered: 774   Skipped: 13

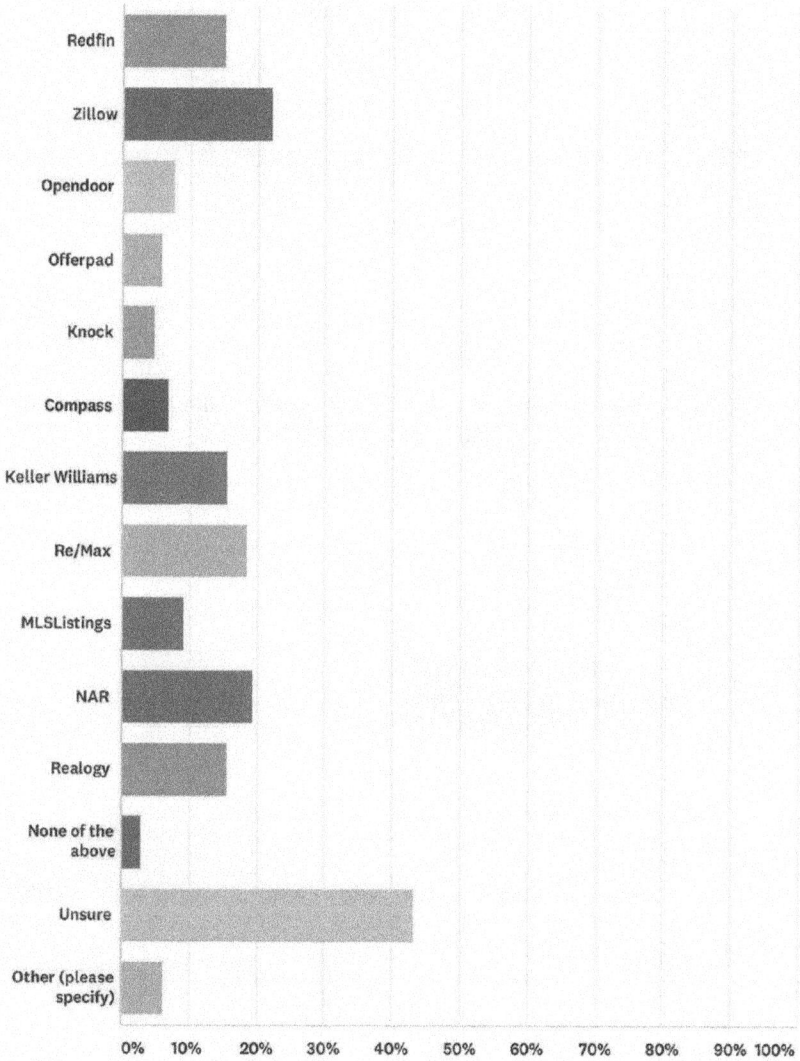

Redfin	
Zillow	
Opendoor	
Offerpad	
Knock	
Compass	
Keller Williams	
Re/Max	
MLSListings	
NAR	
Realogy	
None of the above	
Unsure	
Other (please specify)	

0% 10% 20% 30% 40% 50% 60% 70% 80% 90% 100%

ANSWER CHOICES	RESPONSES	
Redfin	15.37%	119
Zillow	22.09%	171
Opendoor	7.75%	60
Offerpad	5.94%	46
Knock	4.91%	38
Compass	6.85%	53
Keller Williams	15.63%	121
Re/Max	18.60%	144
MLSListings	9.17%	71
NAR	19.38%	150
Realogy	15.76%	122
None of the above	2.97%	23
Unsure	43.28%	335
Other (please specify)	6.20%	48
Total Respondents: 774		

Q31 I believe an attempt to take back control of the industry's listing data from consumer websites is:

Answered: 774   Skipped: 13

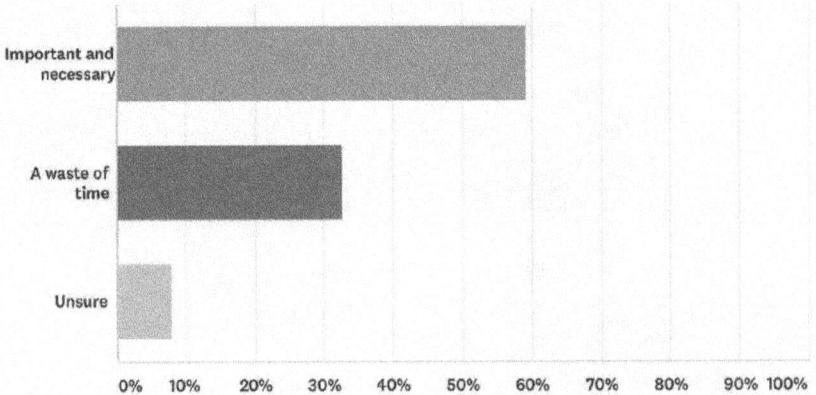

ANSWER CHOICES	RESPONSES	
Important and necessary	59.30%	459
A waste of time	32.69%	253
Unsure	8.01%	62
TOTAL		774

Q32 What would you like to see from leadership at NAR? (Check all that apply.)

Answered: 774   Skipped: 13

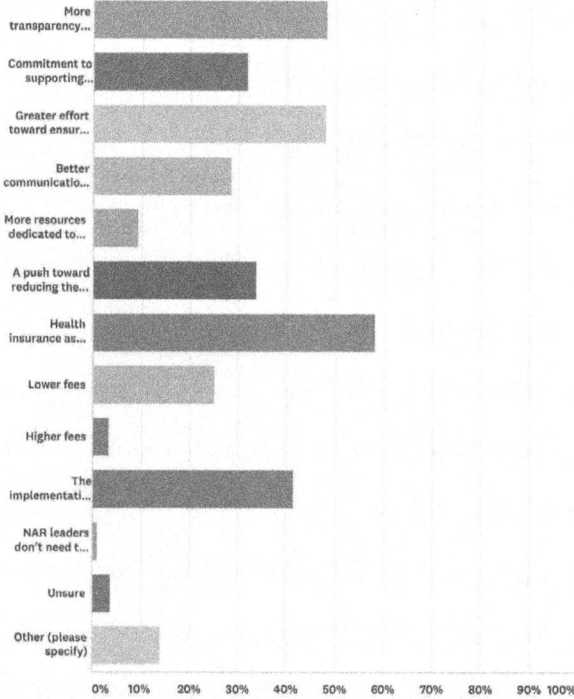

ANSWER CHOICES	RESPONSES	
More transparency about what it does with association funds	48.19%	373
Commitment to supporting in-house technological innovation	31.78%	246
Greater effort toward ensuring third-party tech innovation benefits Realtors	47.80%	370
Better communication regarding upcoming initiatives	28.55%	221
More resources dedicated to political advocacy	9.17%	71
A push toward reducing the number of MLSs nationwide	33.72%	261
Health insurance as a Realtor benefit	58.14%	450
Lower fees	25.19%	195
Higher fees	3.36%	26
The implementation of professionalism requirements	41.47%	321
NAR leaders don't need to change a thing	1.03%	8
Unsure	3.75%	29
Other (please specify)	14.08%	109
Total Respondents: 774		

190

Q33 What would you like to see from your local and state association leadership this year? (Check all that apply.)

Answered: 774   Skipped: 13

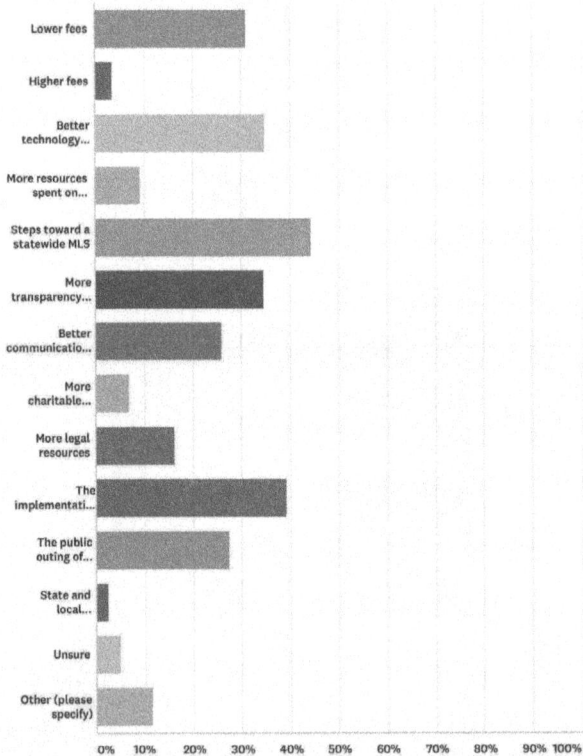

ANSWER CHOICES	RESPONSES	
Lower fees	30.88%	239
Higher fees	3.62%	28
Better technology offerings	34.63%	268
More resources spent on political advocacy	9.17%	71
Steps toward a statewide MLS	44.44%	344
More transparency about what they do with association funds	34.50%	267
Better communication regarding upcoming initiatives	25.97%	201
More charitable events	6.85%	53
More legal resources	16.02%	124
The implementation of professionalism requirements	39.02%	302
The public outing of ethics violators	27.39%	212
State and local association leaders don't need to change a thing	2.45%	19
Unsure	5.04%	39
Other (please specify)	11.50%	89
Total Respondents: 774		

Q34 Should real estate leaders support Realtors Property Resource (RPR)?

Answered: 774   Skipped: 13

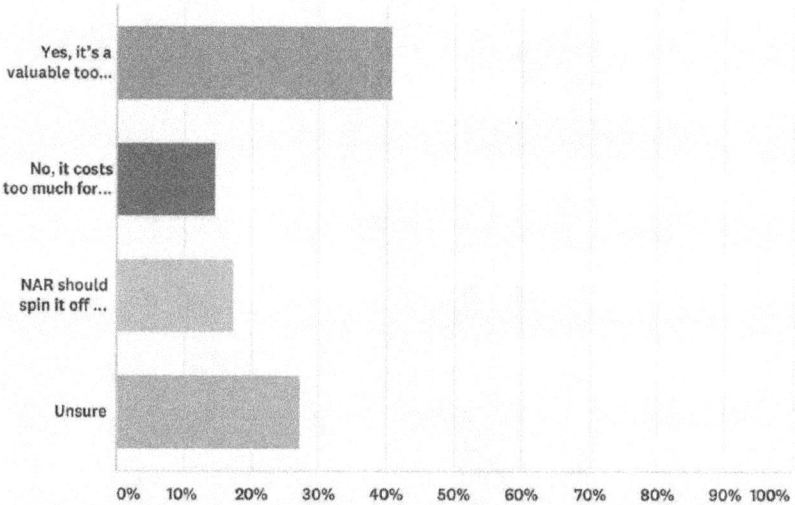

ANSWER CHOICES	RESPONSES	
Yes, it's a valuable tool and only costs about $20 per year per Realtor	40.70%	315
No, it costs too much for what it offers and most Realtors don't use it	14.73%	114
NAR should spin it off and have agents who like the tool pay for it directly	17.44%	135
Unsure	27.13%	210
TOTAL		774

Q35 Should real estate leaders support Upstream once it launches?

Answered: 774   Skipped: 13

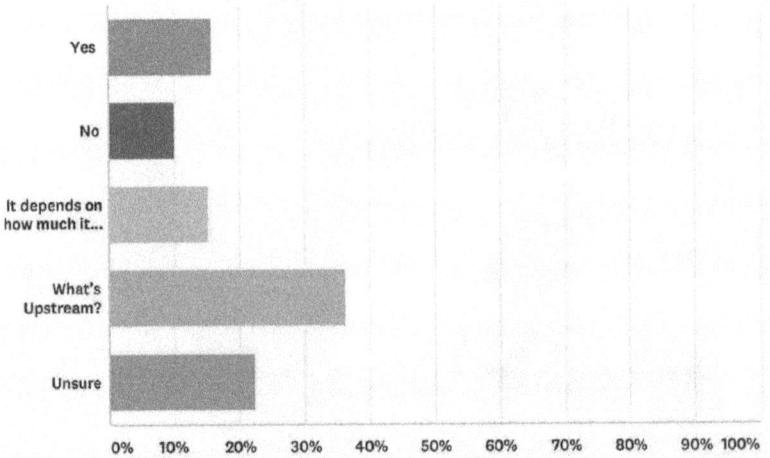

ANSWER CHOICES	RESPONSES	
Yes	15.89%	123
No	10.08%	78
It depends on how much it costs.	15.37%	119
What's Upstream?	36.18%	280
Unsure	22.48%	174
TOTAL		774

Q36 Should real estate leaders try to resist Zillow's influence?

Answered: 774   Skipped: 13

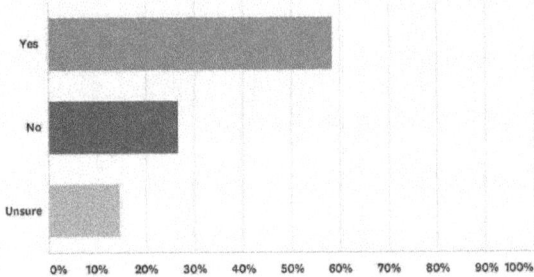

ANSWER CHOICES	RESPONSES	
Yes	58.53%	453
No	26.74%	207
Unsure	14.73%	114
TOTAL		774

Q37 Should real estate leaders fight for a national MLS?

Answered: 774   Skipped: 13

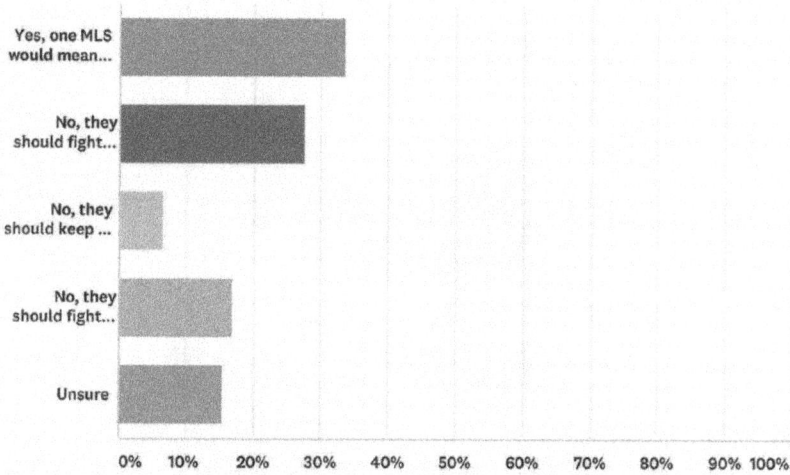

ANSWER CHOICES	RESPONSES	
Yes, one MLS would mean fewer fees, only one set of rules to follow and a national comprehensive database	33.46%	259
No, they should fight to reduce the number of MLSs, but not for a national one	27.52%	213
No, they should keep the current system as is	6.59%	51
No, they should fight for a national MLS database, but keep local governance intact	16.93%	131
Unsure	15.50%	120
TOTAL		774

Q38 What would you like to see from MLS leadership this year? (Check all that apply.)

Answered: 774   Skipped: 13

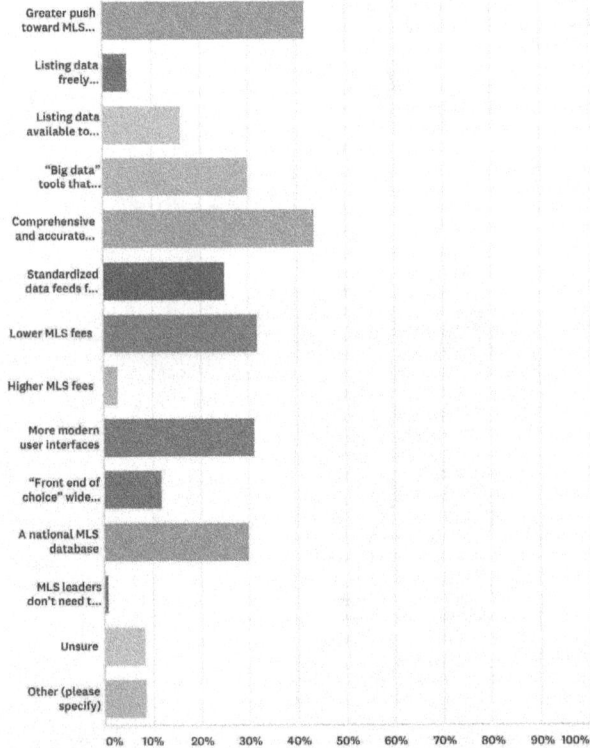

ANSWER CHOICES	RESPONSES	
Greater push toward MLS mergers	41.73%	323
Listing data freely available to tech companies	5.04%	39
Listing data available to tech companies under certain conditions	16.02%	124
"Big data" tools that offer business insights	29.84%	231
Comprehensive and accurate public and private property data	43.54%	337
Standardized data feeds for brokers and tech companies	25.19%	195
Lower MLS fees	31.78%	246
Higher MLS fees	2.97%	23
More modern user interfaces	31.27%	242
"Front end of choice" widely available	11.89%	92
A national MLS database	29.97%	232
MLS leaders don't need to change a thing	0.78%	6
Unsure	8.40%	65
Other (please specify)	8.66%	67
Total Respondents: 774		

Q39 The biggest threat to real estate today is:

Answered: 774   Skipped: 13

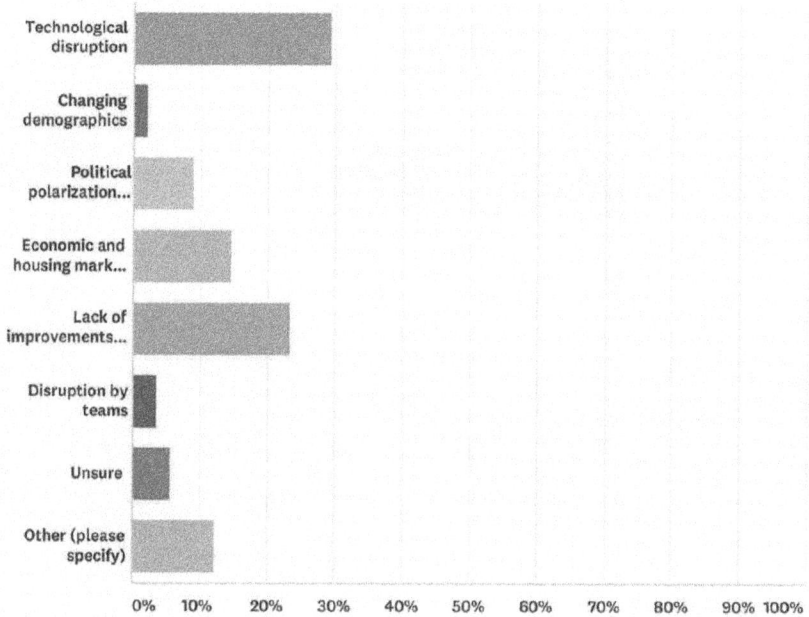

ANSWER CHOICES	RESPONSES	
Technological disruption	29.33%	227
Changing demographics	2.20%	17
Political polarization and global uncertainty	8.91%	69
Economic and housing market changes	14.60%	113
Lack of improvements to the traditional business model	23.39%	181
Disruption by teams	3.62%	28
Unsure	5.56%	43
Other (please specify)	12.40%	96
TOTAL		774

Q40 How well do you think your leadership understands new trends shaping your business?

Answered: 774   Skipped: 13

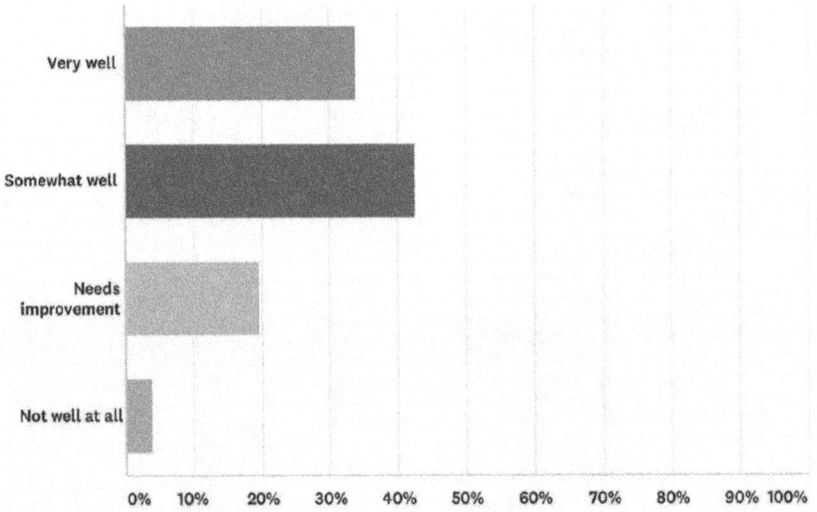

ANSWER CHOICES	RESPONSES	
Very well	33.98%	263
Somewhat well	42.38%	328
Needs improvement	19.64%	152
Not well at all	4.01%	31
TOTAL		774

Q41 How well do you believe your leader understands the needs of new generations of clients and business partners, such as millennials and Gen Z?

Answered: 774   Skipped: 13

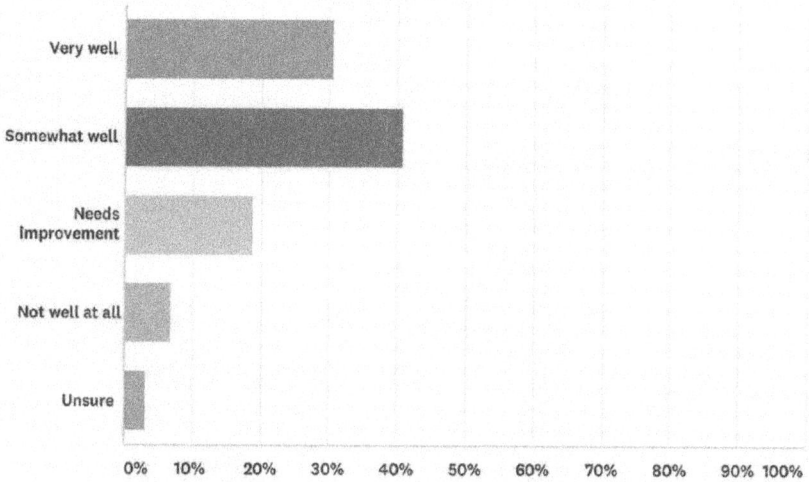

ANSWER CHOICES	RESPONSES	
Very well	30.49%	236
Somewhat well	40.83%	316
Needs improvement	18.73%	145
Not well at all	6.85%	53
Unsure	3.10%	24
TOTAL		774

Q42 Do you think your leadership should be more or less public-facing (appearing on TV, local press, online, live events, etc)?

Answered: 774   Skipped: 13

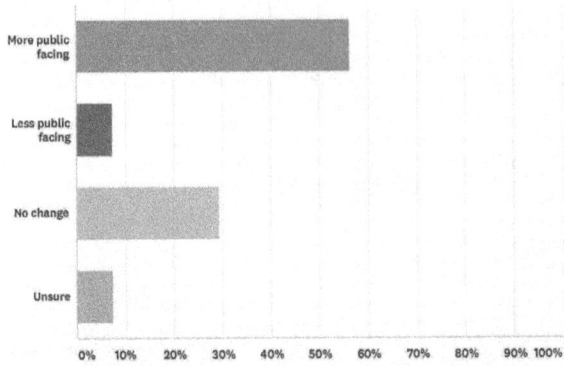

ANSWER CHOICES	RESPONSES	
More public facing	56.20%	435
Less public facing	7.24%	56
No change	29.20%	226
Unsure	7.36%	57
TOTAL		774

Q44 Do you think your leadership should support social causes through your business?

Answered: 767   Skipped: 20

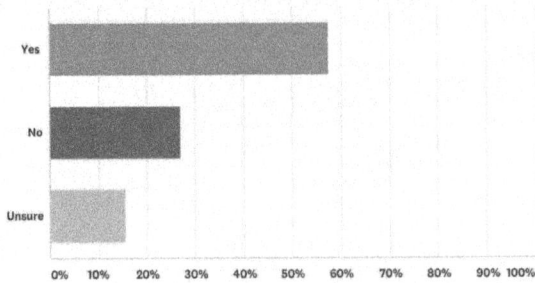

ANSWER CHOICES	RESPONSES	
Yes	57.50%	441
No	26.99%	207
Unsure	15.51%	119
TOTAL		767

Q45 Does your leadership do enough to offer assistance or aid in response to natural disasters?

Answered: 767   Skipped: 20

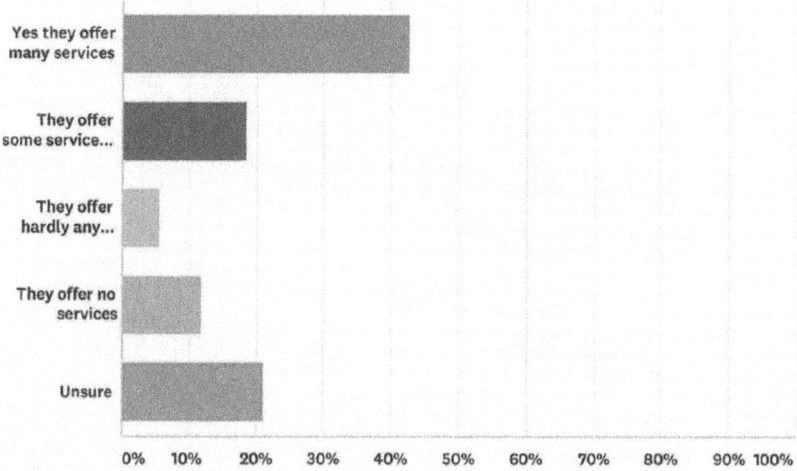

ANSWER CHOICES	RESPONSES	
Yes they offer many services	42.63%	327
They offer some services but could offer more	18.64%	143
They offer hardly any services	5.74%	44
They offer no services	11.86%	91
Unsure	21.12%	162
TOTAL		767

Q46 What are the biggest social and economic issues affecting the real estate industry right now? (Check all that apply.)

Answered: 767   Skipped: 20

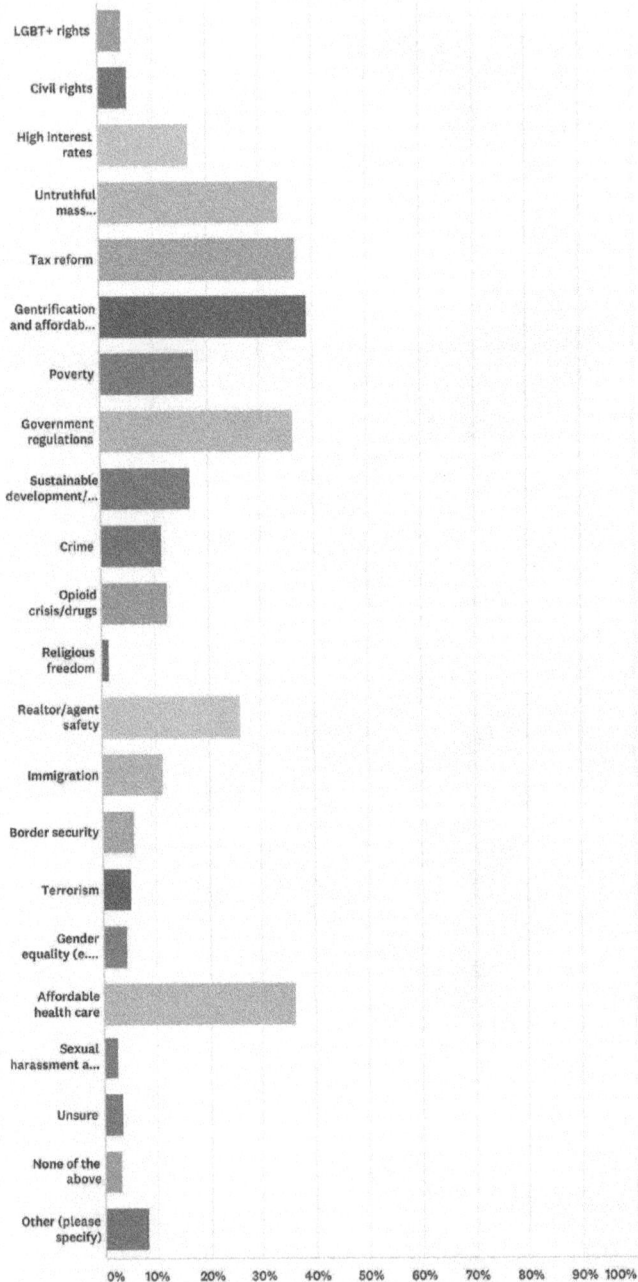

LGBT+ rights
Civil rights
High interest rates
Untruthful mass...
Tax reform
Gentrification and affordab...
Poverty
Government regulations
Sustainable development/...
Crime
Opioid crisis/drugs
Religious freedom
Realtor/agent safety
Immigration
Border security
Terrorism
Gender equality (e....
Affordable health care
Sexual harassment a...
Unsure
None of the above
Other (please specify)

0% 10% 20% 30% 40% 50% 60% 70% 80% 90% 100%

ANSWER CHOICES	RESPONSES	
LGBT+ rights	4.43%	34
Civil rights	5.35%	41
High interest rates	16.69%	128
Untruthful mass media/internet rumors	33.77%	259
Tax reform	36.90%	283
Gentrification and affordable housing	38.98%	299
Poverty	17.60%	135
Government regulations	36.25%	278
Sustainable development/climate change	16.82%	129
Crime	11.21%	86
Opioid crisis/drugs	12.26%	94
Religious freedom	1.56%	12
Realtor/agent safety	26.08%	200
Immigration	11.34%	87
Border security	6.13%	47
Terrorism	5.35%	41
Gender equality (e.g. equal pay)	4.69%	36
Affordable health care	36.11%	277
Sexual harassment and misconduct (#MeToo)	2.74%	21
Unsure	3.52%	27
None of the above	3.26%	25
Other (please specify)	8.34%	64
Total Respondents: 767		

Q47 What social and economic issues has your leadership taken a stand on? (Check all that apply.)

Answered: 767   Skipped: 20

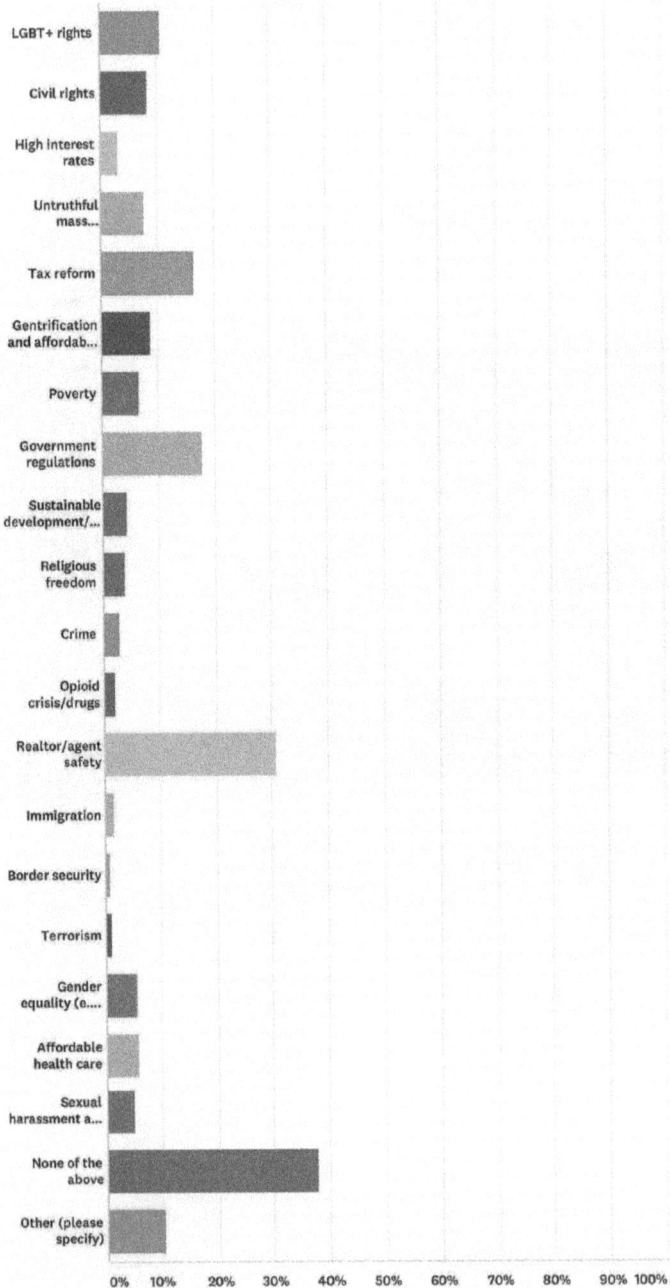

ANSWER CHOICES	RESPONSES	
LGBT+ rights	10.69%	82
Civil rights	8.34%	64
High interest rates	3.13%	24
Untruthful mass media/internet rumors	7.82%	60
Tax reform	16.56%	127
Gentrification and affordable housing	8.87%	68
Poverty	6.65%	51
Government regulations	17.86%	137
Sustainable development/climate change	4.30%	33
Religious freedom	4.04%	31
Crime	2.87%	22
Opioid crisis/drugs	2.09%	16
Realtor/agent safety	30.77%	236
Immigration	1.69%	13
Border security	0.91%	7
Terrorism	1.04%	8
Gender equality (e.g. equal pay)	5.74%	44
Affordable health care	5.87%	45
Sexual harassment and misconduct (#MeToo)	4.95%	38
None of the above	37.94%	291
Other (please specify)	10.43%	80
Total Respondents: 767		

Q48 What social causes do you wish your leadership would take a stand on that they have not yet? (Check all that apply.)

Answered: 767   Skipped: 20

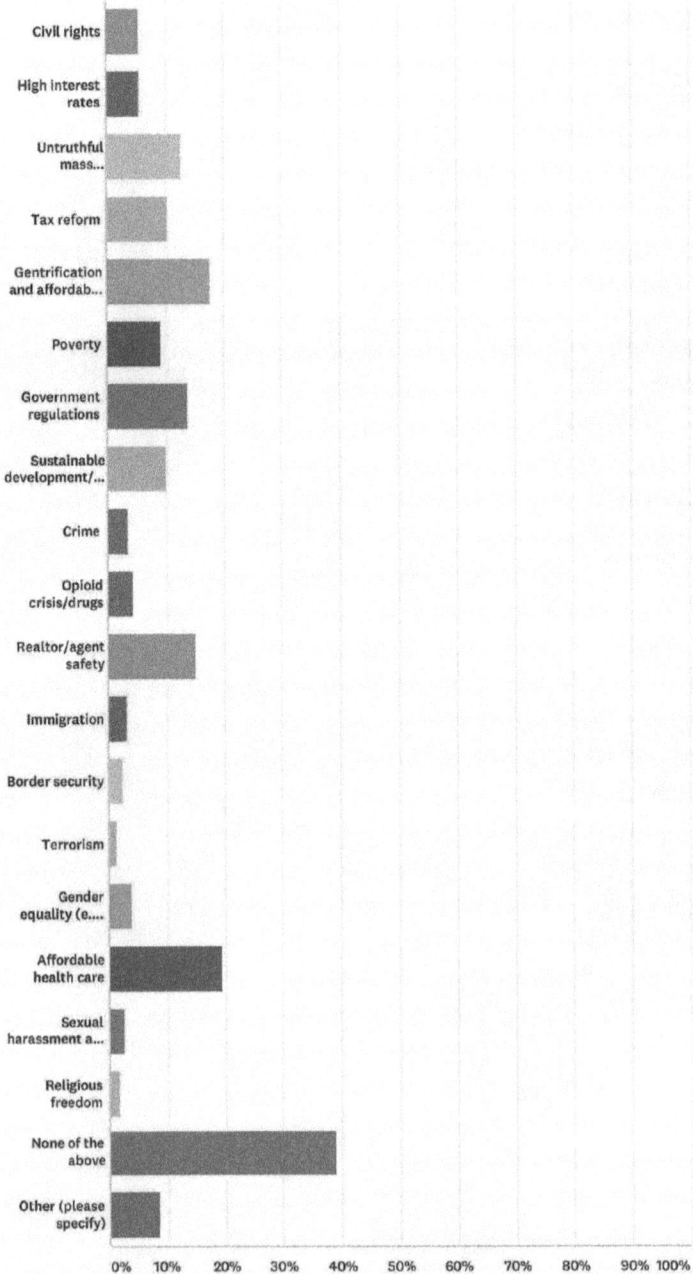

ANSWER CHOICES	RESPONSES	
Civil rights	5.61%	43
High interest rates	5.61%	43
Untruthful mass media/internet rumors	12.78%	98
Tax reform	10.43%	80
Gentrification and affordable housing	17.86%	137
Poverty	9.26%	71
Government regulations	13.82%	106
Sustainable development/climate change	10.04%	77
Crime	3.65%	28
Opioid crisis/drugs	4.30%	33
Realtor/agent safety	14.99%	115
Immigration	3.39%	26
Border security	2.48%	19
Terrorism	1.43%	11
Gender equality (e.g. equal pay)	4.04%	31
Affordable health care	19.43%	149
Sexual harassment and misconduct (#MeToo)	2.74%	21
Religious freedom	1.83%	14
None of the above	38.98%	299
Other (please specify)	8.47%	65
Total Respondents: 767		

Q49 Do you believe your leadership supports or shares your political views?

Answered: 767   Skipped: 20

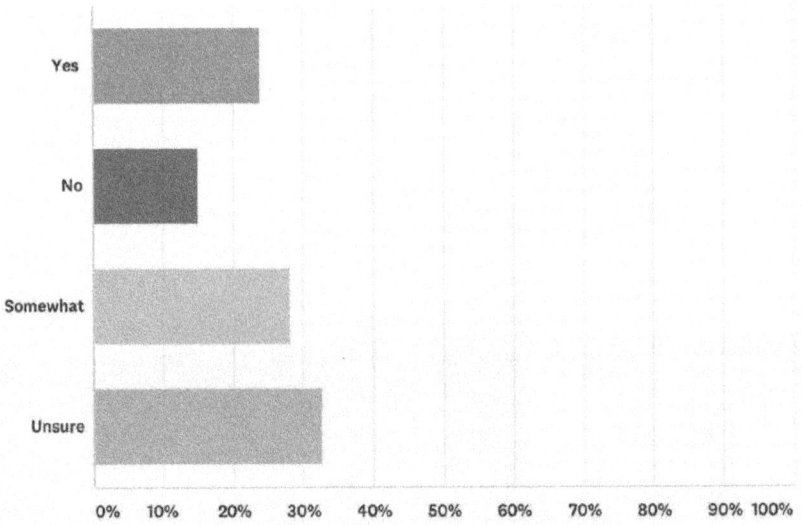

ANSWER CHOICES	RESPONSES	
Yes	24.12%	185
No	15.12%	116
Somewhat	28.16%	216
Unsure	32.59%	250
TOTAL		767

Q50 How important to you is it that your company's leadership reflect the social issues affecting you or that you care about?

Answered: 767   Skipped: 20

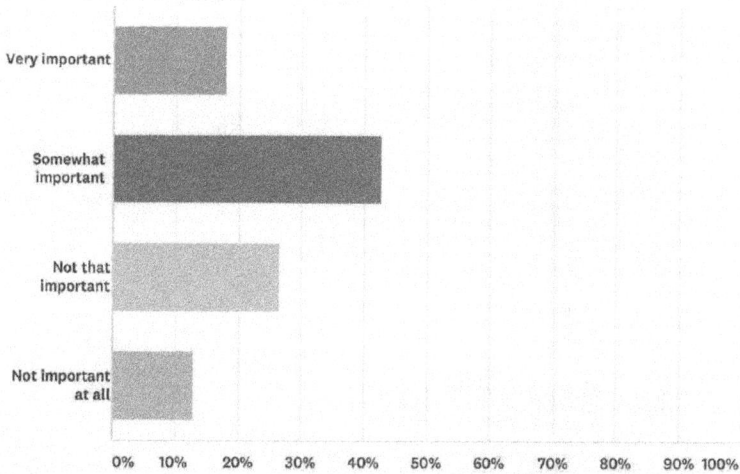

ANSWER CHOICES	RESPONSES	
Very important	17.99%	138
Somewhat important	42.63%	327
Not that important	26.47%	203
Not important at all	12.91%	99
TOTAL		767

Q51 Do you think it's acceptable for leaders to bring up political, religious, or social stances in the workplace or when conducting business?

Answered: 767   Skipped: 20

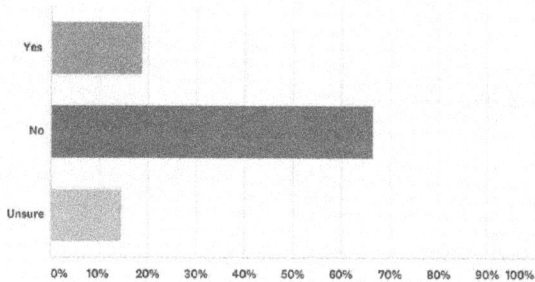

ANSWER CHOICES	RESPONSES	
Yes	18.90%	145
No	66.49%	510
Unsure	14.60%	112
TOTAL		767

Q52 How should the real estate industry work to improve society? (Check all that apply.)

Answered: 787   Skipped: 20

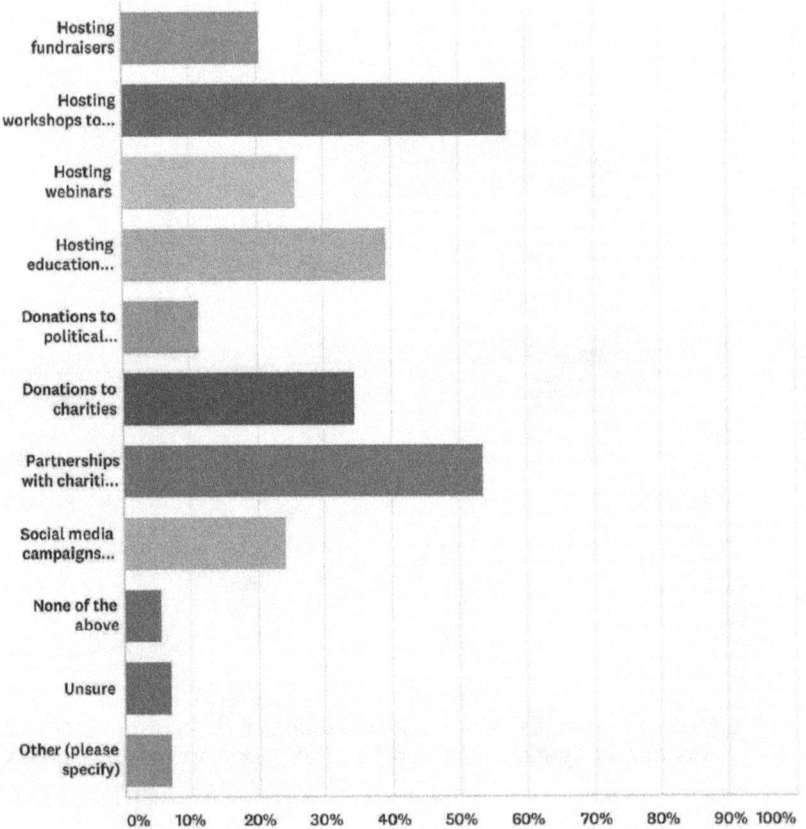

ANSWER CHOICES	RESPONSES	
Hosting fundraisers	20.73%	159
Hosting workshops to educate consumers/clients	57.37%	440
Hosting webinars	25.95%	199
Hosting education seminars for its workforce	39.37%	302
Donations to political candidates or causes	11.60%	89
Donations to charities	34.42%	264
Partnerships with charities or other philanthropic organizations	53.46%	410
Social media campaigns (hashtags)	24.25%	186
None of the above	5.61%	43
Unsure	7.17%	55
Other (please specify)	7.17%	55
Total Respondents: 767		

Q53 Should real estate leaders endorse political candidates?

Answered: 767   Skipped: 20

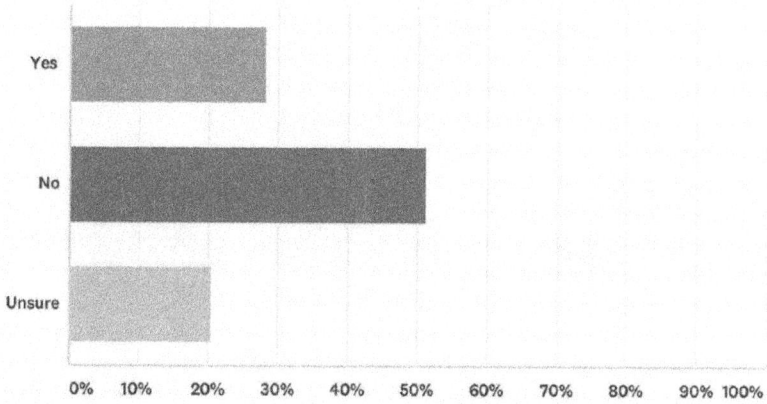

ANSWER CHOICES	RESPONSES	
Yes	28.29%	217
No	51.24%	393
Unsure	20.47%	157
TOTAL		767

Q55 Which best describes your job title?

Answered: 764   Skipped: 23

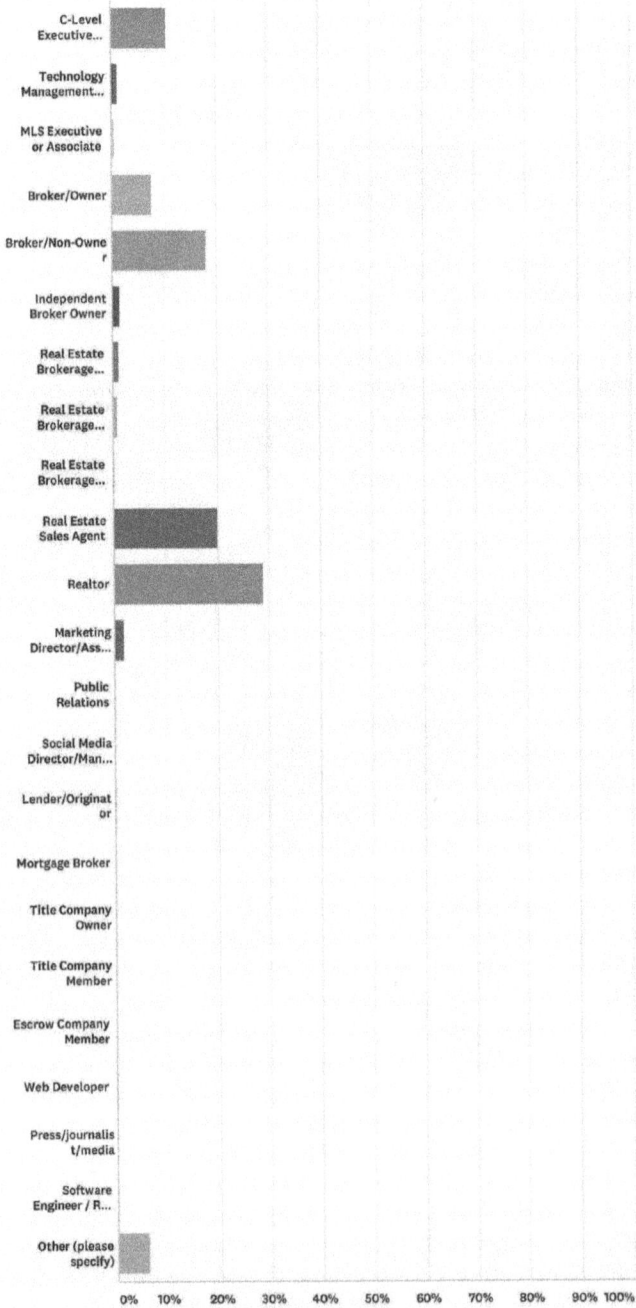

Bar chart with categories (top to bottom): C-Level Executive..., Technology Management..., MLS Executive or Associate, Broker/Owner, Broker/Non-Owner, Independent Broker Owner, Real Estate Brokerage..., Real Estate Brokerage..., Real Estate Brokerage..., Real Estate Sales Agent, Realtor, Marketing Director/Ass..., Public Relations, Social Media Director/Man..., Lender/Originator, Mortgage Broker, Title Company Owner, Title Company Member, Escrow Company Member, Web Developer, Press/journalist/media, Software Engineer / R..., Other (please specify). X-axis: 0% to 100%.

ANSWER CHOICES	RESPONSES	
C-Level Executive Management (CEO, COO, CFO, Owner, Partner, etc)	10.86%	83
Technology Management (CIO, CTO, IT Director, etc.)	1.18%	9
MLS Executive or Associate	0.52%	4
Broker/Owner	7.72%	59
Broker/Non-Owner	18.19%	139
Independent Broker Owner	1.44%	11
Real Estate Brokerage Franchise Owner	1.18%	9
Real Estate Brokerage Franchise Executive	0.92%	7
Real Estate Brokerage Marketing Team Member	0.13%	1
Real Estate Sales Agent	20.03%	153
Realtor	28.93%	221
Marketing Director/Associate	1.83%	14
Public Relations	0.26%	2
Social Media Director/Manager	0.13%	1
Lender/Originator	0.26%	2
Mortgage Broker	0.00%	0
Title Company Owner	0.00%	0
Title Company Member	0.00%	0
Escrow Company Owner	0.00%	0
Escrow Company Member	0.00%	0
Web Developer	0.13%	1
Press/journalist/media	0.00%	0
Software Engineer / Real Estate IT	0.26%	2
Other (please specify)	6.02%	46
TOTAL		764

Q56 What type of company do you work for? (check one)

Answered: 764   Skipped: 23

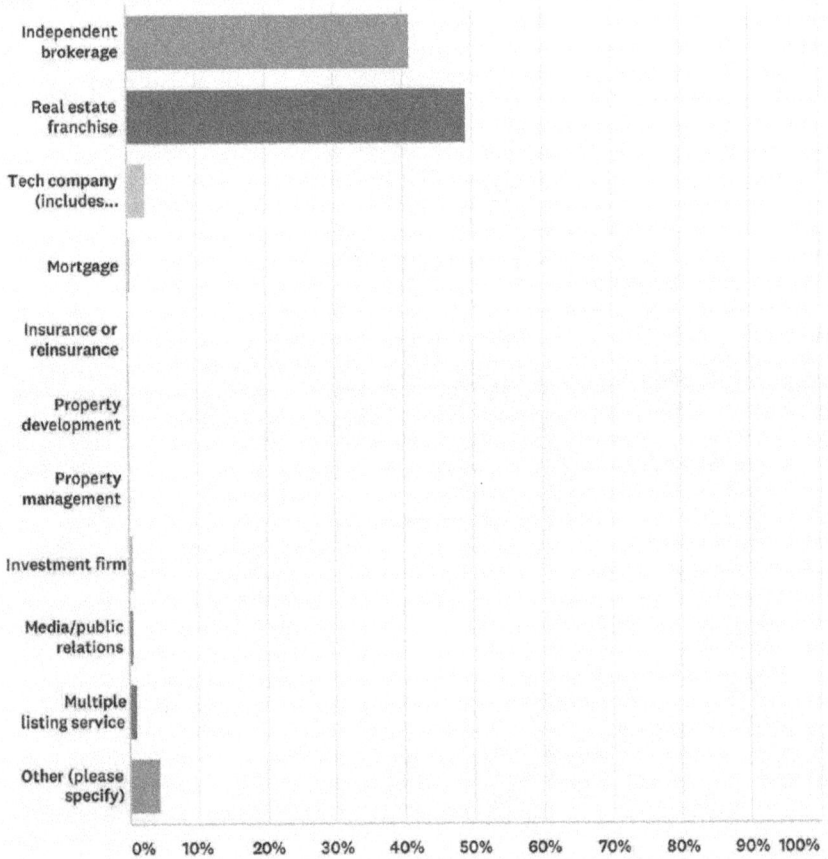

ANSWER CHOICES	RESPONSES	
Independent brokerage	40.97%	313
Real estate franchise	49.21%	376
Tech company (includes software and startups)	2.62%	20
Mortgage	0.39%	3
Insurance or reinsurance	0.00%	0
Property development	0.13%	1
Property management	0.13%	1
Investment firm	0.52%	4
Media/public relations	0.52%	4
Multiple listing service	1.05%	8
Other (please specify)	4.45%	34
TOTAL		764

Q58 What is the size of your company?

Answered: 764   Skipped: 23

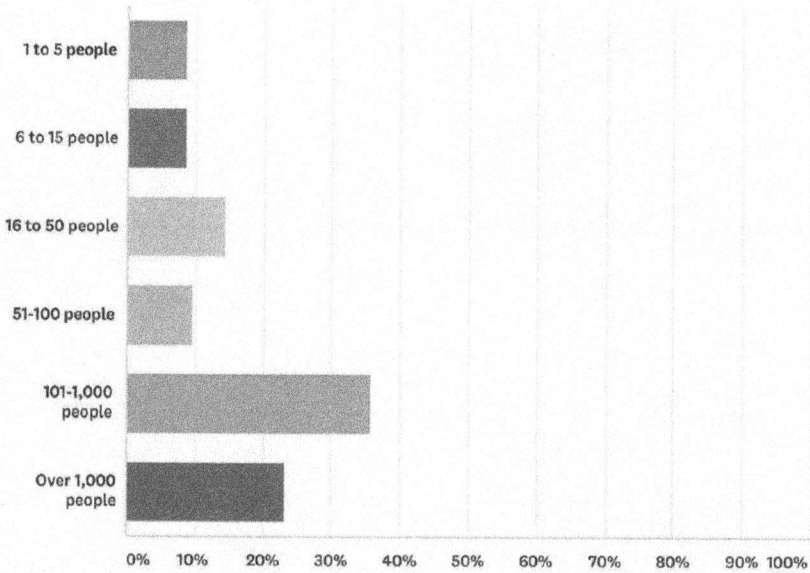

ANSWER CHOICES	RESPONSES	
1 to 5 people	8.64%	66
6 to 15 people	8.51%	65
16 to 50 people	14.40%	110
51-100 people	9.55%	73
101-1,000 people	35.73%	273
Over 1,000 people	23.17%	177
TOTAL		764

Q59 How many years have you been licensed in real estate?

Answered: 764   Skipped: 23

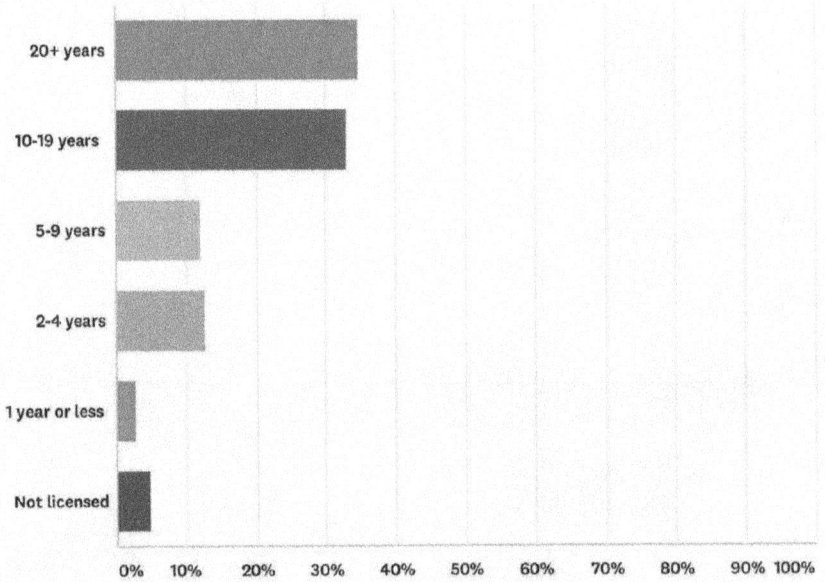

ANSWER CHOICES	RESPONSES	
20+ years	34.69%	265
10-19 years	32.98%	252
5-9 years	12.17%	93
2-4 years	12.70%	97
1 year or less	2.75%	21
Not licensed	4.71%	36
TOTAL		764

Q60 If your primary role is to sell real estate, what was your/your team's overall production in 2017?

Answered: 764   Skipped: 23

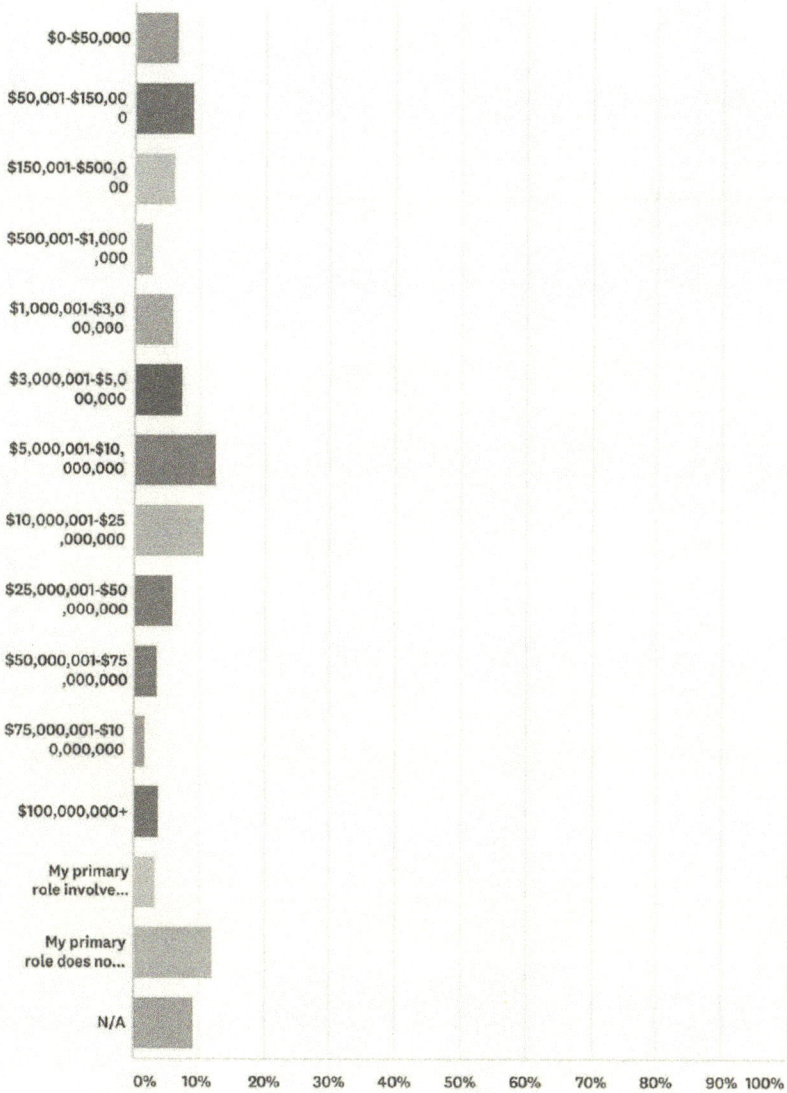

$0-$50,000	
$50,001-$150,000	
$150,001-$500,000	
$500,001-$1,000,000	
$1,000,001-$3,000,000	
$3,000,001-$5,000,000	
$5,000,001-$10,000,000	
$10,000,001-$25,000,000	
$25,000,001-$50,000,000	
$50,000,001-$75,000,000	
$75,000,001-$100,000,000	
$100,000,000+	
My primary role involve...	
My primary role does no...	
N/A	

0% 10% 20% 30% 40% 50% 60% 70% 80% 90% 100%

ANSWER CHOICES	RESPONSES	
$0-$50,000	6.41%	49
$50,001-$150,000	8.90%	68
$150,001-$500,000	6.02%	46
$500,001-$1,000,000	2.75%	21
$1,000,001-$3,000,000	5.89%	45
$3,000,001-$5,000,000	7.33%	56
$5,000,001-$10,000,000	12.57%	96
$10,000,001-$25,000,000	10.73%	82
$25,000,001-$50,000,000	5.89%	45
$50,000,001-$75,000,000	3.53%	27
$75,000,001-$100,000,000	1.57%	12
$100,000,000+	3.80%	29
My primary role involves real estate sales, but I was not selling actively in 2017	3.40%	26
My primary role does not involves real estate sales	12.04%	92
N/A	9.16%	70
TOTAL		764